EXCEL
BUILD THE TOOLS
YOU REALLY NEED

INTRODUCTION

Welcome to this Excel training course! In this book, you'll (re)-discover the basics of the famous software, and the main aim is to help you make the links with your day-to-day use.

In the long run, using Excel correctly can save you a considerable amount of time in your work, whatever your sector.

The whole course is practical: just open Excel ...

Prices and company names are used in the projects: everything is of course fictitious, the aim being to understand the mechanisms.

The course is made up of nine independent projects, in ascending order of difficulty: each project has its own subject and correction, and the files are specified in the introduction to each one.

This book is based on the 2023 version of Microsoft 365 for Business: some functions may evolve or be moved depending on the version, so don't hesitate to search the Internet for these elements.

To retrieve the files, please go to the link given at the end of the book, then download the folder by clicking on the icon.

Unzip the downloaded .zip file, and you're ready to go!

FLOUR BUSINESS

On this first project, you have been asked to compare the selling prices of flour from different suppliers.

Each of them has sent you a proposal, which you'll find in document "01 - Subject consultations.pdf".

An example of a correction is the file :
"01 - Correction Consultations.xlsx"

Create a new Excel file, and here we go!

Flour price per tonne

Farinella	Crossroad Flour	Flour Passport	Farina
685,00 €	632,00 €	695,00 €	636,00 €
1 353,00 €	1 303,00 €	1 369,00 €	1 393,00 €
4 285,00 €	4 249,00 €	4 252,00 €	4 258,00 €
682,00 €	704,00 €	742,00 €	671,00 €
566,00 €	592,00 €	540,00 €	506,00 €

Quantity (T)	Minimal price per tonne	Total
5	632,00 €	3 160,00 €
6	1 303,00 €	7 818,00 €
8,5	4 215,00 €	35 827,50 €
9,6	671,00 €	6 441,60 €
7	506,00 €	3 542,00 €

Order Total :	56 789,10 €

Covered concepts :
Formulas, table, cell formatting, conditional formatting, MIN(), MAX() and AVERAGE(), graphics.

FLOUR BUSINESS

To start with, we need to enter the values of the quotes in the same table.

From B4 to F4, enter the names of the 5 given suppliers.

Flour Affiliate	Farinella	Crossroad Flour	Flour Passport	Farina

From A5 to A9, enter the 5 different flours.
You can enter "References" in A4.

	A
1	
2	
3	
4	References
5	Wheat flour
6	Rye flour
7	Oat flour
8	Spelt flour
9	Buckwheat flour

FLOUR BUSINESS

This double-entry table can now be used to fill in the prices given in the quotations.

From the PDF file, fill in the price for each flour per tonne for each supplier.

Please note: some prices are given "per Tonne" and therefore require no calculation, but others are given in kg, in which case you'll need to enter a calculation in the box.

Here's an example for wheat flour from Farine Affiliate:

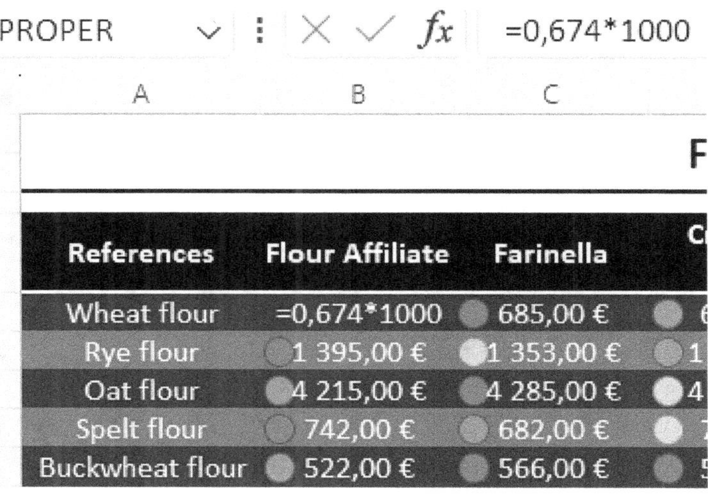

The prices are fairly close, so an error will be easily detected once the table has been completed.

FLOUR BUSINESS

Excel offers a function that makes it easier to exploit data once it's been executed: table formatting.

To do this, click on a cell in your table, then go to "Insert - Table";

The following window appears:

Excel suggests a default data range. If the data to be inserted in your table is not the one you want to use, you can select the range yourself.

Here, the "My table has headers" box is ticked: these will be my suppliers. If your table doesn't have headers, unchecking this box will create them automatically.

Click on "Ok".

FLOUR BUSINESS

Click on your table, then go to the "Table Design" tab.

You'll find a wide range of formatting options to suit your taste!

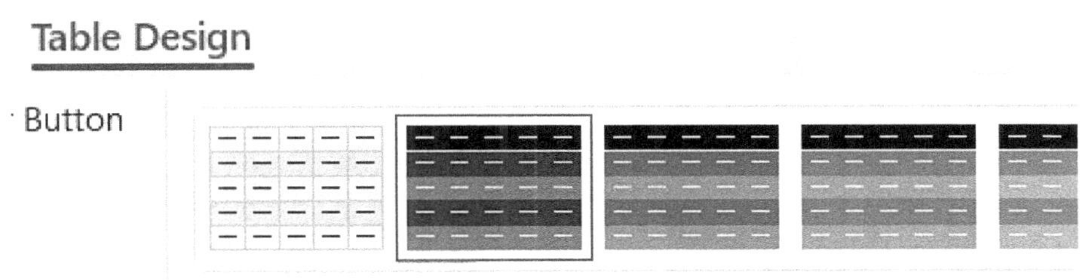

The values displayed are in the classic number format; to transform them into $, select cells B5 to I9 then click on the drop-down list in the "Number" section of the "Home" tab. Choose "Currency".

FLOUR BUSINESS

Excel's conditional formatting feature uses colors to highlight differences in the data.

We're going to apply conditional formatting to each flour. To do this, select the line from B5 to F5, then click on "Conditional formatting" :

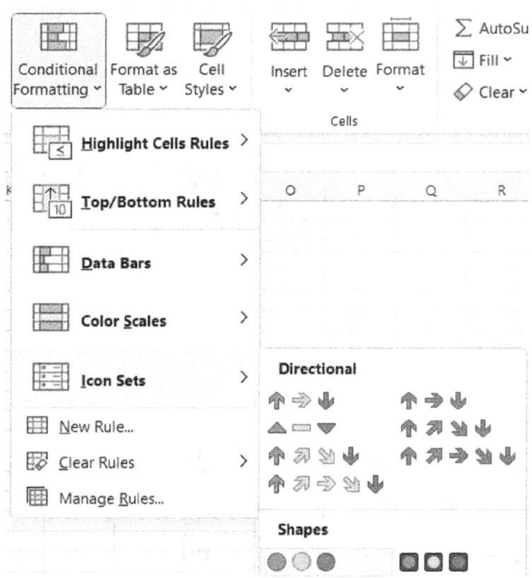

Select the shapes , then click on "Manage rules", then on your created rule to click on "Reverse icon order": this way, red is the most expensive and green the cheapest!

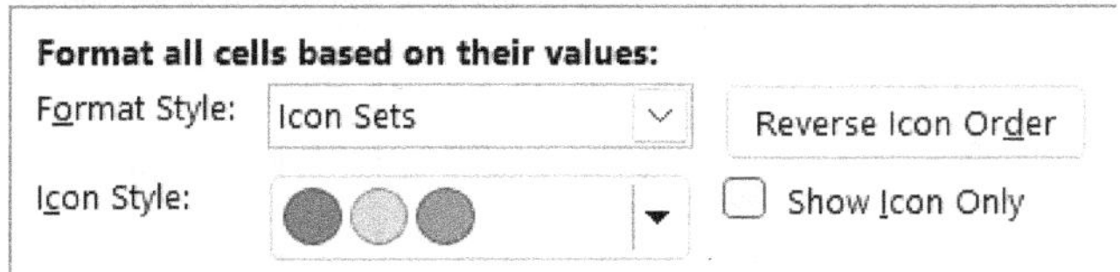

Repeat for all lines (B6 to F6, etc).

FLOUR BUSINESS

While conditional formatting gives us visual information on price trends, it's still time-consuming to search for a precise value.

In cell **G9**, enter "Minimum price", then enter the formula **=MIN()** :

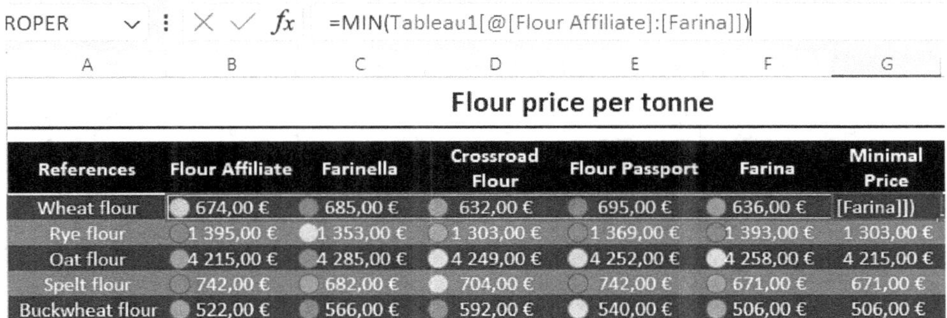

	Flour price per tonne					
References	Flour Affiliate	Farinella	Crossroad Flour	Flour Passport	Farina	Minimal Price
Wheat flour	674,00 €	685,00 €	632,00 €	695,00 €	636,00 €	[Farina]])
Rye flour	1 395,00 €	1 353,00 €	1 303,00 €	1 369,00 €	1 393,00 €	1 303,00 €
Oat flour	4 215,00 €	4 285,00 €	4 249,00 €	4 252,00 €	4 258,00 €	4 215,00 €
Spelt flour	742,00 €	682,00 €	704,00 €	742,00 €	671,00 €	671,00 €
Buckwheat flour	522,00 €	566,00 €	592,00 €	540,00 €	506,00 €	506,00 €

Once the **=MIN(** formula has been entered, select cells **B5 to F5** for the function to be filled in: Excel will calculate the minimum price for the range indicated.

When you press "Enter", the formula automatically scrolls to the bottom of the table, thanks to the conversion into a table made earlier.

Minimal Price
632,00 €
1 303,00 €
4 215,00 €
671,00 €
506,00 €

FLOUR BUSINESS

We'll perform the same type of calculation to obtain the maximum price.

In cell H9, enter "Maximum price" and then enter the formula =MAX() :

```
=MAX(Tableau1[@[Flour Affiliate]:[Farina]])
```

Flour price per tonne

Farinella	Crossroad Flour	Flour Passport	Farina	Minimal Price	Maximal Price
685,00 €	632,00 €	695,00 €	636,00 €	632,00 €	[Farina]])
1 353,00 €	1 303,00 €	1 369,00 €	1 393,00 €	1 303,00 €	1 395,00 €
4 285,00 €	4 249,00 €	4 252,00 €	4 258,00 €	4 215,00 €	4 285,00 €
682,00 €	704,00 €	742,00 €	671,00 €	671,00 €	742,00 €
566,00 €	592,00 €	540,00 €	506,00 €	506,00 €	592,00 €

Once the =MAX(formula has been entered, select cells B5 to F5 for the function to be filled in: Excel will calculate the minimum price for the range indicated.

When you press "Enter", the formula automatically scrolls to the bottom of the table.

Maximal Price
695,00 €
1 395,00 €
4 285,00 €
742,00 €
592,00 €

FLOUR BUSINESS

Once again, we'll perform the same type of calculation to obtain the average price.

In cell I9, enter "Average price" and then enter the formula =AVERAGE() :

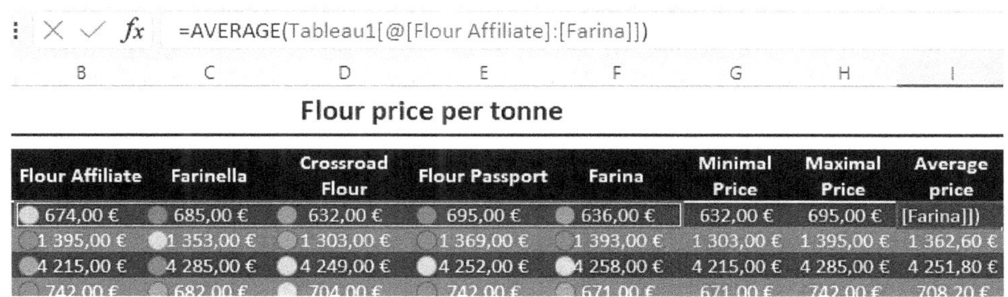

Flour Affiliate	Farinella	Crossroad Flour	Flour Passport	Farina	Minimal Price	Maximal Price	Average price
674,00 €	685,00 €	632,00 €	695,00 €	636,00 €	632,00 €	695,00 €	[Farina]])
1 395,00 €	1 353,00 €	1 303,00 €	1 369,00 €	1 393,00 €	1 303,00 €	1 395,00 €	1 362,60 €
4 215,00 €	4 285,00 €	4 249,00 €	4 252,00 €	4 258,00 €	4 215,00 €	4 285,00 €	4 251,80 €
742,00 €	682,00 €	704,00 €	742,00 €	671,00 €	671,00 €	742,00 €	708,20 €

Once the =AVERAGE(formula has been entered, select cells B5 to F5 for the function to be filled in: Excel will calculate the average price for the range indicated.

When you press "Enter", the formula automatically scrolls to the bottom of the table.

Average price
664,40 €
1 362,60 €
4 251,80 €
708,20 €
545,20 €

FLOUR BUSINESS

Now that our table is ready, we'll place an order for flour. We want to know the price for the following quantities, based on the minimum price :

Order	
Wheat flour	5000 kg
Rye flour	6 T
Oat flour	8500kg
Spelt flour	9600 kg
Buckwheat flour	7 T

You can work on the Excel sheet to try to find the total price of the order; there are several methods, so don't look at the correction example straight away.

Here's what a correction might look like:

Order		Quantity (T)	Minimal price per tonne	Total
Wheat flour	5000 kg	5	632,00 €	3 160,00 €
Rye flour	6 T	6	1 303,00 €	7 818,00 €
Oat flour	8500kg	8,5	4 215,00 €	35 827,50 €
Spelt flour	9600 kg	9,6	671,00 €	6 441,60 €
Buckwheat flour	7 T	7	506,00 €	3 542,00 €
			Order Total :	56 789,10 €

The first step is to convert everything into tons, then bring back the minimum prices; finally, multiply the quantity by the price (=Quantity*Price) then sum the totals (=SUM(E13:E17) in this example).

FLOUR BUSINESS

You'd like to zoom in on rye flour to share with your partners. A graph would facilitate communication.

Select cells B6 to F6, then insert a column chart from the "Insert" tab:

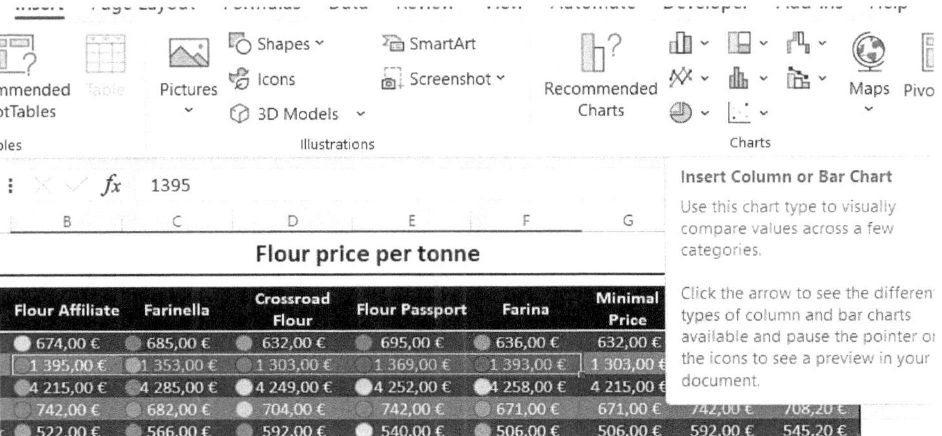

In the "Graphic creation" and "Formatting" tabs, work on your new graphic to create a clear, easy-to-use display. Here's an example:

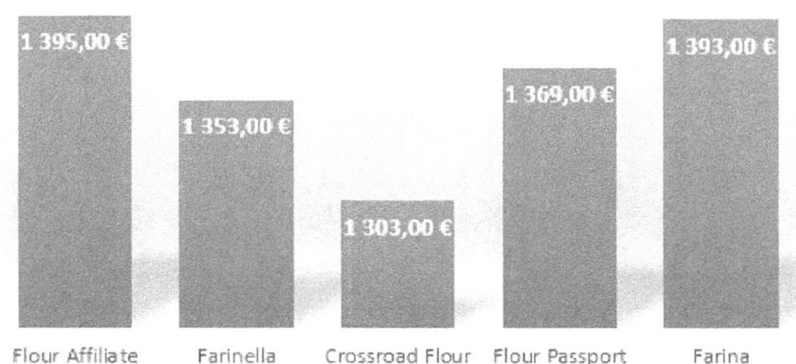

FLOUR BUSINESS

To conclude this little study, you can work on the overall formatting of your document:

- **Title size**
- **Cell fills**
- **Borders**

The clearer and more usable your document is, the more useful you'll be to anyone who might need to consult it, especially your "future you"!

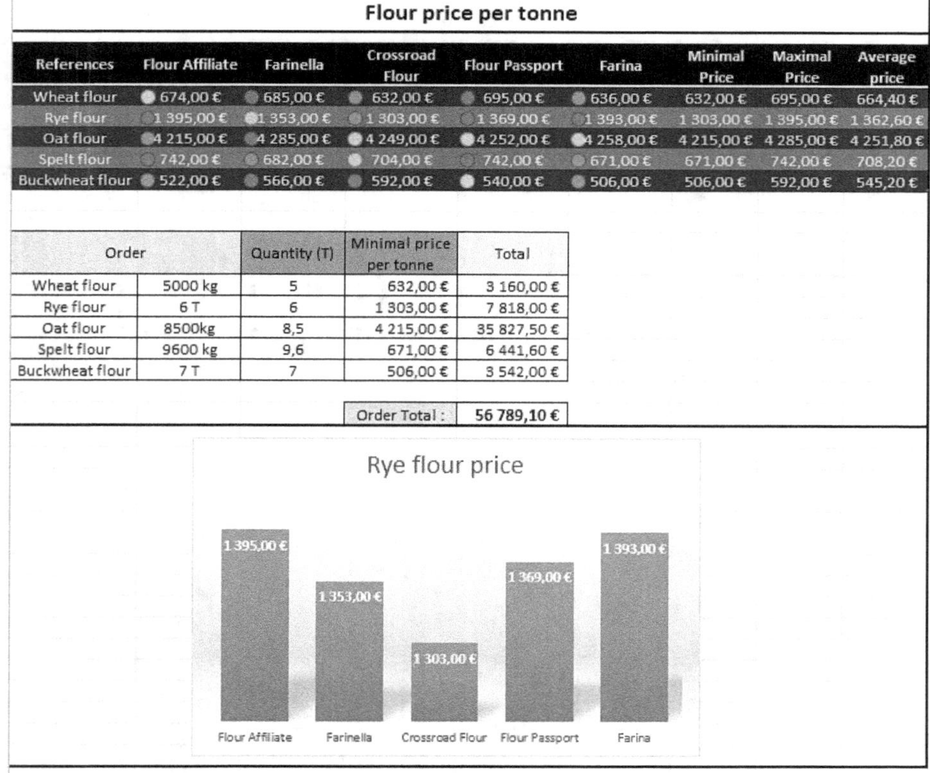

References	Flour Affiliate	Farinella	Crossroad Flour	Flour Passport	Farina	Minimal Price	Maximal Price	Average price
				Flour price per tonne				
Wheat flour	674,00 €	685,00 €	632,00 €	695,00 €	636,00 €	632,00 €	695,00 €	664,40 €
Rye flour	1 395,00 €	1 353,00 €	1 303,00 €	1 369,00 €	1 393,00 €	1 303,00 €	1 395,00 €	1 362,60 €
Oat flour	4 215,00 €	4 285,00 €	4 249,00 €	4 252,00 €	4 258,00 €	4 215,00 €	4 285,00 €	4 251,80 €
Spelt flour	742,00 €	682,00 €	704,00 €	742,00 €	671,00 €	671,00 €	742,00 €	708,20 €
Buckwheat flour	522,00 €	566,00 €	592,00 €	540,00 €	506,00 €	506,00 €	592,00 €	545,20 €

Order	Quantity (T)	Minimal price per tonne	Total
Wheat flour	5000 kg	5	632,00 €	3 160,00 €
Rye flour	6 T	6	1 303,00 €	7 818,00 €
Oat flour	8500kg	8,5	4 215,00 €	35 827,50 €
Spelt flour	9600 kg	9,6	671,00 €	6 441,60 €
Buckwheat flour	7 T	7	506,00 €	3 542,00 €

Order Total :	56 789,10 €

PRODUCTS EVERYWHERE

For this second project, you want to operate a database containing no fewer than 1,000 products.

For each product, information is given such as packaging, package volume and price per country.

An example of a correction is the file :
"02 - Correction Base price by country.xlsx".

The base file is "02 - Subject Base price by country.xlsx".

	A	B	C	D	E	F	G	H
1								
2		Packaging	Packaging volume (m3)	France	Italy	Spain	Germany	Portugal
3	Product1	50	0,9	39	96	32	80	30
4	Product2	50	1,2	85	94	70	39	60
5	Product3	10	0,8	71	57	25	88	92
6	Product4	30	1,2	53	97	90	71	83
7	Product5	80	0,5	22	42	100	90	55
8	Product6	80	1,1	37	44	60	88	13
9	Product7	10	1,1	68	48	35	22	28
10	Product8	30	1,2	23	16	58	67	48
11	Product9	100	0,5	86	16	16	61	25
12	Product10	20	0,7	12	44	57	76	72
13	Product11	80	0,6	51	46	83	27	39
14	Product12	50	1,2	31	65	62	62	17
15	Product13	10	1	99	42	82	79	71
16	Product14	10	0,6	65	71	79	96	92
17	Product15	10	0,6	86	43	35	19	80
18	Product16	10	1,2	42	27	71	19	67
19	Product17	20	1,1	42	81	49	90	96
20	Product18	10	1,2	73	22	14	32	28
21	Product19	50	0,7	82	69	84	51	13
22	Product20	70	0,9	61	49	55	17	50
23	Product21	40	1,2	65	18	51	60	95
24	Product22	20	1,1	16	86	25	14	62
25	Product23	60	1,2	70	88	37	52	12
26	Product24	70	0,9	59	56	14	75	56
27	Product25	60	0,8	65	14	36	16	23
28	Product26	50	1	57	38	19	12	47
29	Product27	80	0,5	56	46	26	19	12
30	Product28	60	1	25	38	25	60	56

Covered concepts :
NBVAL(), IF(), conditional formatting, MIN(), INDEX/MATCH, VLOOKUP().

PRODUCTS EVERYWHERE

To begin with, we want to know how many items our list contains.

The first solution would be to scroll down to the last item and count the rows, but this won't give us the evolution of the number of items.
Moreover, we need a sentence like "There are X products".

Place yourself in N2, then write the following formula:

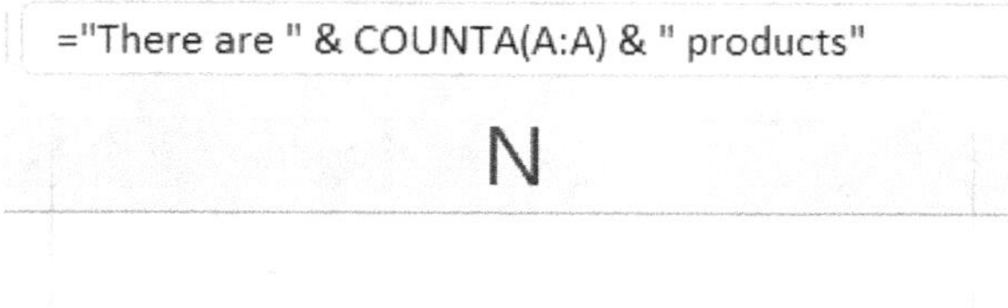

The function **COUNTA(A:A)** counts the number of non-empty cells in column A, i.e. the number of products here.

On the other hand, you've inserted text and a formula in the same cell. If you try to delete or add a product, your number will be updated automatically.

PRODUCTS EVERYWHERE

Packaging in column B is either 1, 10, 50 or 100 units. For ease of use, we'd like to show whether a pack is "Unit" or "Grouped".

Right-click on column C, then "Insert".

In cell C3, enter the following formula:

```
=IF(B3=1;"Unit";"Grouped")
```

The IF function allows you to perform a test (in this case, is cell B3 equal to 1?), then returns the value if the test is passed (in this case, "Unit"), or the value if the test is not passed (in this case, "Grouped").

To extend the formula, place your cursor at the bottom-right corner of C3 and double-click: the formula extends to the bottom of the workbook!

Packaging	Packaging Type
50	Grouped
50	Grouped
10	Grouped
1	Unit
1	Unit
1	Unit
10	Grouped

PRODUCTS EVERYWHERE

Once again, we're going to apply the "IF" formula, as it's often used in Excel. This time, we're going to look at the type of volume: if it's greater than 1m3, then it will be noted as "Large", otherwise as "Small".

Right-click on column E, then "Insert".
In cell E3, enter the following formula:

$$fx \quad =IF(D6>1;\text{"Large"};\text{"Small"})$$

The IF function performs a test (in this case, is cell D3 greater than 1?), then returns the value if the test is met (in this case, "Voluminous"), or the value if the test is not met (in this case, " Small").

You can test in any way you like; for example, the test might be to see if cell D3 is less than 1, in which case the last two arguments will be reversed.

To extend the formula, place your cursor at the bottom-right corner of E3 and double-click.

Packaging volume (m3)	Volume type
0,9	Small
1,2	Large
0,8	Small
1,2	Large
0,5	Small
1,1	Large

PRODUCTS EVERYWHERE

To make the packaging types stand out more clearly, we can apply conditional formatting to the text.

Select cell C3, then Ctrl + Shift + Down arrow to select all values. Click on "Conditional formatting" - "New rule".

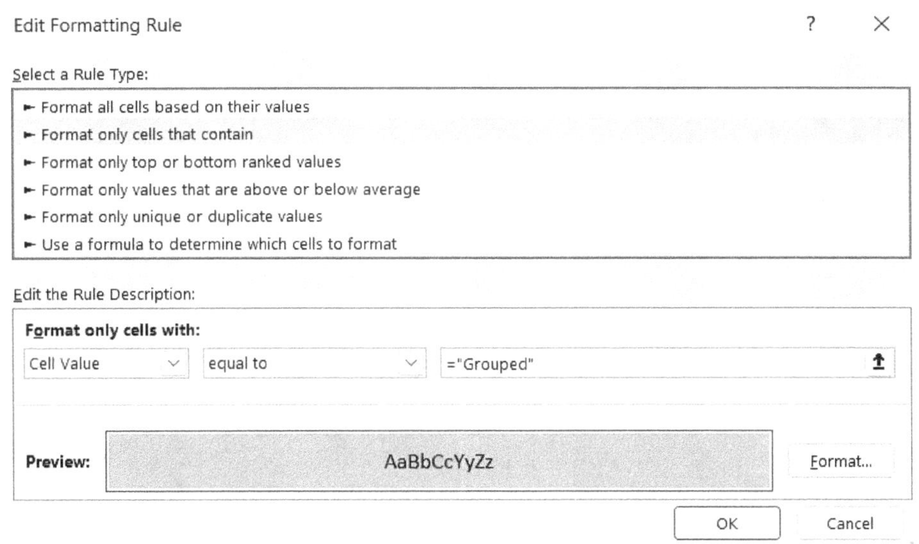

On the window that appears, fill in the elements as above; the format is a yellow fill for grouped packaging. When you confirm, all boxes containing "Grouped" are yellow.

You can repeat the operation for "Unit" with a green fill, for example.

PRODUCTS EVERYWHERE

To make the volume types stand out more clearly, we can apply conditional formatting to the text.

Select cell E3, then Ctrl + Shift + Down arrow to select all values. Click on "Conditional Formatting" - "New Rule".

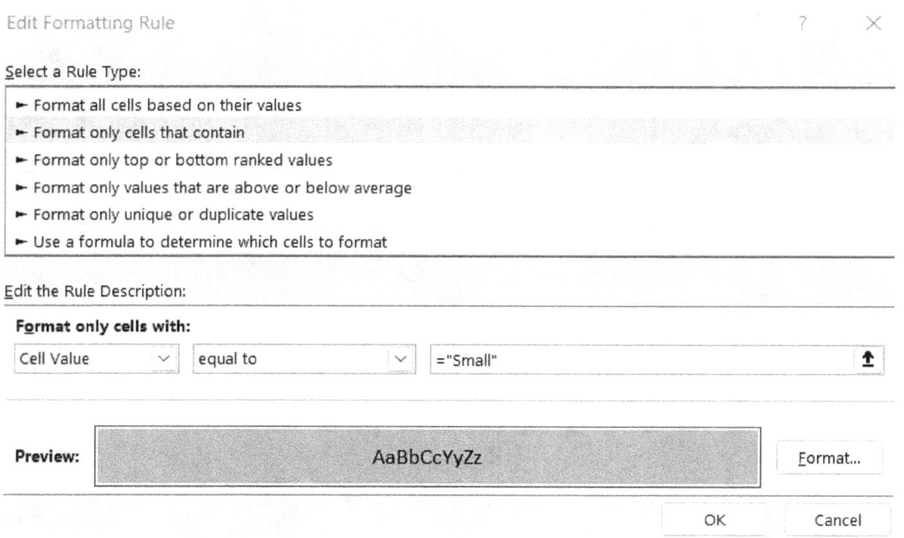

On the window that appears, fill in the elements as above; the format is a green fill for a " Small" element. When you confirm, all boxes containing "Small" are green.

You can repeat the operation for " Voluminous " with a red fill, for example.

PRODUCTS EVERYWHERE

Next, our analysis will require us to show the minimum price for each product.

In K2, enter "Minimum price", then enter the following formula in K3 :

fx =MIN(F3:J3)

K
Minimum price
30
39
25
53
22

Place your cursor at the bottom right of cell K3, then double-click to extend the formula to the bottom.

Next, we want to show which country offers this cheapest price. In L2, enter "Cheapest country", then go to the next page...

Minimum price	Cheapest country

PRODUCTS EVERYWHERE

The set of formulas shown here is widely used, but seems rather laborious at first sight.

Select cell L3, then enter the following formula:

fx `=INDEX($F$2:$J$2;1;MATCH(K3;F3:J3;0))`

The index formula returns a position in an array. Here, the array $F$2:$J$2 is the list of countries. The second argument is the line of the returned array: it has only one line, number 1. Finally, the column returned will depend on the minimum price calculated earlier: this is the MATCH() function.

MATCH() returns the position of a value in a range. Here, we're looking for the minimum price (K3) in the price range (F3:J3) to return its position, which will be the column in INDEX(), i.e. the country providing this minimum price.

The $ are used to "lock" the cells: here, $ are used on the country table, as values from this table will always be returned.

You can then extend the formula :

Minimum price	Cheapest country
30	Portugal
39	Germany
25	Spain
53	France
22	France
13	Portugal
22	Germany

PRODUCTS EVERYWHERE

While we've made this document more readable, it's still time-consuming to quickly obtain information on a particular product.

The aim here is to create a search engine using the **VLOOKUP()** function.

In cells **N6** to **O10**, create the following table:

Product search :	
Packaging	
Packaging Type	
Minimum Price	
Cheapest country	

In box **O7**, enter the following formula:

fx =VLOOKUP($O$6;A:B;2;FALSE)

The **VLOOKUP()** formula searches for the value of cell **O6** in the value range formed by columns **A** and **B**. Once the value has been found, we ask you to return the 2nd column. The **"FALSE"** argument indicates that the search is for the exact value entered.

The search range (here **A:B**) must contain both the value searched for and the value returned, otherwise an error will occur.

PRODUCTS EVERYWHERE

Here's a second example of **VLOOKUP()**, this time for cell O8, i.e. the volume type:

$$fx \quad =VLOOKUP(\$O\$6;A:E;5;FALSE)$$

For each item in the table, write the **VLOOKUP()** to find the right information.

Then test your search engine by trying out other product values to see how powerful your tool is!

Product search :	Product563
Packaging	10
Packaging Type	Large
Minimum Price	18
Cheapest country	Italy

ON THE ROAD

For this third project, you want to operate a database containing data on trucks.

Each truck has a reference, a purchase date, a purchase cost and a type. The aim is to analyze this data.

An example of a correction is the file :
"03 - Database trucks.xlsx"

The base file is "03 - Subject Database trucks.xlsx".

GESTION DES CAMIONS

Référence	Date d'achat	Coût d'acha	Type de camic
Camion119	2021	41 403,00 €	Citerne
Camion344	2022	15 617,00 €	Benne
Camion267	2023	41 304,00 €	Plateau
Camion5	2023	26 314,00 €	Benne
Camion202	2023	29 100,00 €	Plateau
Camion362	2022	48 220,00 €	Citerne
Camion81	2020	49 346,00 €	Malaxeur
Camion399	2021	21 556,00 €	Benne
Camion39	2023	44 174,00 €	Plateau
Camion458	2023	23 466,00 €	Plateau
Camion280	2022	15 064,00 €	Plateau
Camion383	2023	31 517,00 €	Plateau
Camion391	2023	36 000,00 €	Plateau
Camion35	2022	19 382,00 €	Plateau
Camion413	2022	30 893,00 €	Plateau
Camion294	2024	18 676,00 €	Plateau
Camion222	2021	37 259,00 €	Citerne
Camion384	2022	20 850,00 €	Citerne
Camion143	2024	40 842,00 €	Plateau
Camion28	2023	16 094,00 €	Plateau
Camion347	2022	25 121,00 €	Citerne
Camion99	2020	40 327,00 €	Plateau
Camion136	2020	24 345,00 €	Benne
Camion36	2023	24 722,00 €	Citerne

Type camion	Nombre
Citerne	88
Benne	73
Plateau	78
Malaxeur	82

Type camion	Achats
Citerne	2 945 805,00 €
Benne	2 198 730,00 €
Plateau	2 402 823,00 €
Malaxeur	2 671 397,00 €

Camion recherché :	Camion402
Date d'achat	2024
Coût	36 332,00 €
Type	Malaxeur

Conditions	Nombre / montant
Malaxeurs avant 2022	34
Plateaux après 2021	59
Citerne en 2020	15
Benne entre 2022 et 2023	33
Achats citerne avant 2023	1 913 938,00 €

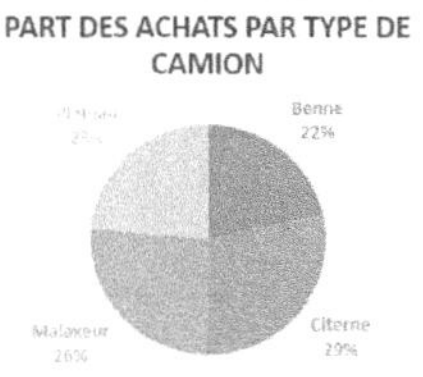

Covered concepts :
Table, cell format, COUNTIF(), SUMIF(), XLOOKUP(), TRANSPOSE(), COUNTIFS(), SUMIFS(), graphics

ON THE ROAD

To begin with, the initial workbook is not very usable in its current form: the first step is to transform it into a table.

Click on A3, then Insert - Table :

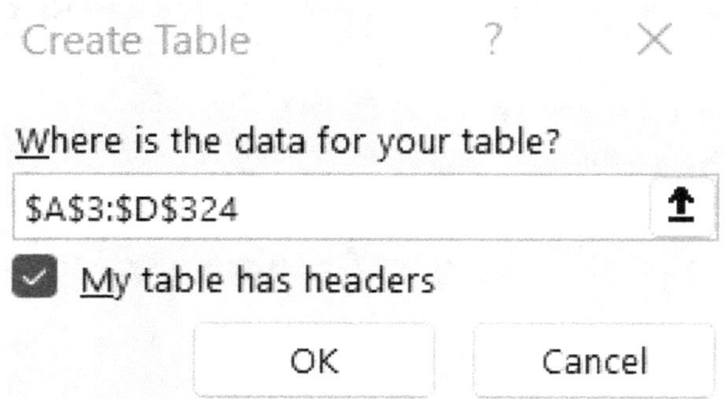

The table starts on the third line and the headers are filled in.

Database Trucks			
Reference	Purchase date	Purchase co	Type
Truck119	2021	$ 41 403,00	Tanker
Truck344	2022	$ 15 617,00	Tipper
Truck267	2023	$ 41 304,00	Flatbed
Truck5	2023	$ 26 314,00	Tipper
Truck202	2023	$ 29 100,00	Flatbed
Truck362	2022	$ 48 220,00	Tanker
Truck81	2020	$ 49 346,00	Mixer
Truck399	2021	$ 21 556,00	Tipper
Truck39	2023	$ 44 174,00	Flatbed
Truck458	2023	$ 23 466,00	Flatbed
Truck280	2022	$ 15 064,00	Flatbed
Truck383	2023	$ 31 517,00	Flatbed
Truck391	2023	$ 36 000,00	Flatbed
Truck35	2022	$ 19 382,00	Flatbed
Truck413	2022	$ 30 893,00	Flatbed
Truck294	2024	$ 18 676,00	Flatbed

ON THE ROAD

To make it easier to read, we're going to transform the data in column C into currency.

Select column C, then in "Home", "Number" category, select " Accounting" :

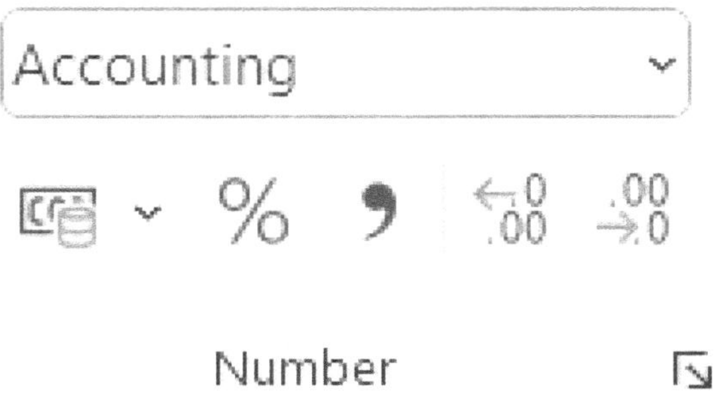

Note: you can choose the number of decimal places to be displayed. Here, we'll display two.

Purchase co ▾
$ 41 403,00
$ 15 617,00
$ 41 304,00
$ 26 314,00
$ 29 100,00
$ 48 220,00
$ 49 346,00
$ 21 556,00
$ 44 174,00

ON THE ROAD

The first analysis will be the number of trucks by type.

From F4 to G8, create the following table:

Type	Number
Tanker	
Tipper	
Flatbed	
Mixer	

In cell G5, write the formula COUNTIF(then select column D. Insert a ";", then click F5 to give the function's second argument.

| | | fx | =COUNTIF(Tableau2[Type];F5) |

st ⌄	Type ⌄		Type	Number
00	Tanker		Tar=COUNTIF(Tableau2[Type];F5)	
00	Tipper		Tipper	73
00	Flatbed		Flatbed	78
00	Tipper		Mixer	82
00	Flatbed			
00	Tanker			

This function adds 1 to each occurrence of the searched value. Here, it is asked to search for "Tanker" in column D, which gives the number of tanker trucks. Extend the formula to obtain the other numbers.

ON THE ROAD

The second analysis will focus on the purchase cost of trucks by type.

From F10 to G14, create the following table:

Type	Total Purchase
Tanker	
Tipper	
Flatbed	
Mixer	

In cell G11, insert the formula SUMIF(by selecting column D (the search range), then cell F11 (the truck type), and finally column C (the purchase cost, i.e. the range to be summed).

`=SUMIF(Tableau2[Type];F11;Tableau2[Purchase cost])`

Database Trucks

irchase date	Purchase cos	Type
2021	$ 41 403,00	Tanker
2022	$ 15 617,00	Tipper
2023	$ 41 304,00	Flatbed
2023	$ 26 314,00	Tipper
2023	$ 29 100,00	Flatbed
2022	$ 48 220,00	Tanker
2020	$ 49 346,00	Mixer
2021	$ 21 556,00	Tipper
2023	$ 44 174,00	Flatbed
2023	$ 23 466,00	Flatbed
2022	$ 15 064,00	Flatbed

Type	Number
Tanker	88
Tipper	73
Flatbed	78
Mixer	82

Type	Total Purchase
Tanker	cost])
Tipper	2 198 730,00 €
Flatbed	2 402 823,00 €
Mixer	2 671 397,00 €

This formula can be used to obtain sums spent by truck type and, more generally, to sum values with a condition.

ON THE ROAD

As in the previous topic, it's quite difficult to find information on a particular truck.

So we're going to build a search engine, but with a different formula.

First, construct the following table from F16 to G19:

Truck search :	
Purchase date	
Purchase cost	
Type	

We will insert the function in G17 :

```
=XLOOKUP(G16;Tableau2[Reference];Tableau2
[[Purchase date]:[Type]];"No match")
```

This function asks you to search for the value of cell G16 ("search bar") in the "Reference" column of the table. It then returns the "Purchase dates", "Purchase cost" and "Truck type" columns. If no match is found, it returns "No match".

Truck search :	Truck402	
Purchase date	2024	36332 Mixer
Purchase cost		
Type		

ON THE ROAD

The difference between **VLOOKUP()** and **XLOOKUP()** lies in the values returned: **VLOOKUP()** returns a single cell, while **XLOOKUP()** returns an entire array.

As we've seen, the returned values appear horizontally; that's not how my array is structured. We'll therefore integrate **=TRANSPOSE(XLOOKUP(...))** to display the results in columns.

```
=TRANSPOSE(XLOOKUP(G16;Tableau2[Reference];Tableau2[[Purchase date]:[Type]];"No match"))
```

	D	E	F	G
6,00	Mixer		Type	Total Purchase
6,00	Tipper		Tanker	2 945 805,00 €
4,00	Flatbed		Tipper	2 198 730,00 €
6,00	Flatbed		Flatbed	2 402 823,00 €
4,00	Flatbed		Mixer	2 671 397,00 €
7,00	Flatbed			
0,00	Flatbed		Truck search :	Truck402
2,00	Flatbed		Purchase date	2024
3,00	Flatbed		Purchase cost	36 332,00 €
6,00	Flatbed		Type	Mixer

The **=TRANSPOSE()** function inverts the rows and columns of a given table.

My search engine is now functional.

ON THE ROAD

We are now going to count values under several conditions.

First, create the following table from F21 to G26:

Criteria	Number / Cost
Mixer before 2022	
Flatbed after 2021	
Tanker in 2020	
Tipper from 2022 to 2023	
Tanker purchase before 2023	

Each of these lines requires the integration of several conditions: the **COUNTIF()** function is not sufficient. **COUNTIFS()** must be used to count the values that satisfy both conditions:

`=COUNTIFS(Tableau2[Type];"Mixer";Tableau2[Purchase date];"<2022")`

F Criteria	G Number / Cost
Mixer before 2022	34
Flatbed after 2021	59
Tanker in 2020	15
Tipper from 2022 to 2023	33

Complete the formulas down to cell G25.

ON THE ROAD

The **COUNTIFS()** function is used to create a counter based on different values.

Here, for **G26**, we need to sum a range according to different criteria (on the same principle as SUMIF()).

Thus, the formula to use is **SUMIFS()**, where we first enter the range to be summed, then the various criteria.

fx =SUMIFS(Tableau2[Purchase cost];Tableau2[Type];"Tipper";Tableau2[Purchase date];"<2023")

Criteria	Number / Cost
Mixer before 2022	34
Flatbed after 2021	59
Tanker in 2020	15
Tipper from 2022 to 2023	33
Tanker purchase before 2023	1 287 519,00 €

ON THE ROAD

To conclude this project, we're going to create a chart to identify which trucks cost the most.

Select cells F11 to G14, then insert a pie chart.

Type	Total Purchase
Tanker	2 945 805,00 €
Tipper	2 198 730,00 €
Flatbed	2 402 823,00 €
Mixer	2 671 397,00 €

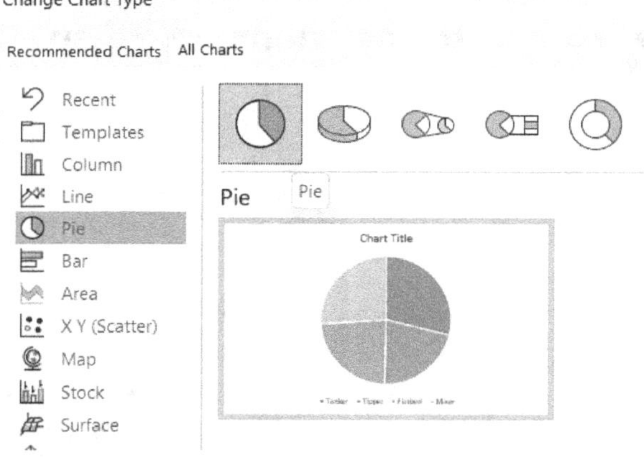

Display percentages and insert title.

LET'S MEET

Already the fourth project! We're going to be able to step up a gear. You start with a file containing data on personnel interviews to be carried out in a company; all the information will have to be centralized.

The basic file is "04 - Subject staff management.xlsx".

An example of a correction is the file :
"04 - Correction staff management.xlsx"

Open the basic file, and off you go!

| | Staff management | | | | | Today | 11/02/23 |

Department	Name	Position	Last interview	Number of months between interviews	Next interview
Plumbing	Armani Dalton	Business manager	08/06/23	3	11/06/23
Tiling	Tyler O'brien	Head of department	09/08/23	2	11/08/23
Tiling	Marcus Conley	Business manager	08/09/23	3	11/09/23
Plumbing	Mathew Puckett	Business manager	08/13/23	3	11/13/23
Plumbing	Gabriel Mayo	Head of department	09/15/23	2	11/15/23
Kitchen	Apollo Heath	Business manager	08/16/23	3	11/16/23
Heating	August Sellers	Business manager	08/24/23	3	11/24/23
Electricity	Declan Gibbs	Business manager	08/25/23	3	11/25/23
Electricity	Ezequiel Avery	Business manager	08/26/23	3	11/26/23
Kitchen	Remy Wilkerson	Business manager	08/26/23	3	11/26/23
Heating	Joel Fowler	Business manager	08/27/23	3	11/27/23
Electricity	Blake Rollins	Head of department	09/28/23	2	11/28/23
Kitchen	Holden William	Head of department	09/28/23	2	11/28/23
Electricity	Lewis Perkins	Business manager	08/31/23	3	11/30/23
Bathroom	Mario Emerson	Head of department	10/07/23	2	12/07/23
Heating	Brendan Meyer	Business manager	09/09/23	3	12/09/23

Interview information

Covered concepts:
VOLLOKUP(), EDATE(), Sorting, TODAY(), conditional formatting, Hyperlinks, workbook protection.

LET'S MEET

In the initial document, create a "General" sheet:

In this new sheet, create a table with the following columns:

- Department
- Name
- Position
- Last interview
- Number of months between interviews
- Next interview

Staff management

Department	Name	Position	Last interview	Number of months between interviews	Next interview

LET'S MEET

In the "General" sheet, enter information from existing pages (by copy/paste) for the following columns:
- **Name**
- **Position**
- **Last interview**
- **Department**

Department	Name	Position	Last interview
Bathroom	Mario Emerson	Head of department	10/07/23
Bathroom	Damon Harrell	Business manager	09/30/23
Bathroom	Stephen Vincent	Designer	07/08/23
Bathroom	Corbin Cohen	Designer	07/08/23
Bathroom	Quinn Mcneil	Business manager	10/25/23
Bathroom	Ruben Salas	Business manager	10/27/23
Bathroom	Adrian Whitehead	Designer	08/01/23
Bathroom	Amari Martinez	Designer	08/05/23
Bathroom	Omari Meyers	Designer	08/15/23

The sheets of each service can be deleted:

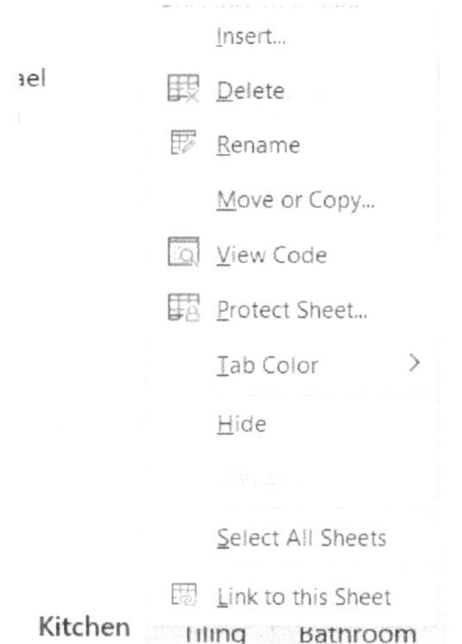

LET'S MEET

If you haven't already done so, create a table via Insert - Table to facilitate data processing.

Depending on their position, employees are not interviewed at the same frequency. We're going to enter this frequency in a new sheet.

Create an "Interview information" sheet, with cells A1 to B4 :

Poste	Number of months between interviews
Head of department	2
Business manager	3
Designer	6

This sheet will be used to calculate the next interview date for each employee.

LET'S MEET

In this section, we'll automatically fill in the "Number of months between interviews" column in the table.

In the case of a new employee, the aim would be not to have to enter this duration, but for it to appear according to the employee's position.

Here's the formula to enter in the first line of the "Number of months between interviews" column:

fx =VLOOKUP([@Position];'Interview information'!$A$2:$B$4;2;FALSE)

The searched value is the cell containing the position, which is searched in the "Interview information" sheet in the range containing the position and the duration.

Position	Last interview	Number of months between interviews
Head of department	10/07/23	2
Business manager	09/30/23	3
Designer	07/08/23	6
Designer	07/08/23	6
Business manager	10/25/23	3
Business manager	10/27/23	3
Designer	08/01/23	6
Designer	08/05/23	6
Designer	08/15/23	6
Designer	09/07/23	6
Designer	09/18/23	6
Designer	10/07/23	6
Designer	10/16/23	6

LET'S MEET

Now that the gap is shown in the table, we can use it to automatically calculate the date of the next interview.

The function used is EDATE(), to be inserted in the first line of the "Next interview" column:

fx | =EDATE([@[Last interview]];[@[Number of months between interviews]])

The function asks for the date to be advanced, and by how many months: the value of the number of months between interviews is collected.

Last interview	Number of months between interviews	Next interview
10/07/23	2	12/07/23
09/30/23	3	12/30/23
07/08/23	6	01/08/24
07/08/23	6	01/08/24
10/25/23	3	01/25/24
10/27/23	3	01/27/24
08/01/23	6	02/01/24
08/05/23	6	02/05/24
08/15/23	6	02/15/24

If the last interview date is changed, the next interview date is automatically updated.

LET'S MEET

The main advantage of this tool is that it allows us to see the order of future interviews; we no longer have to go through each page of each service line by line, but we can see which interviews are coming up next.

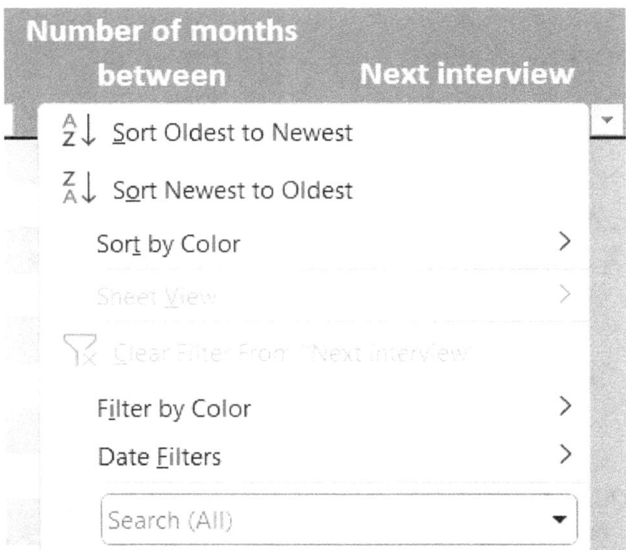

On the "Next interview" header, choose the sorting order from oldest to newest, and your dates will appear in order of urgency.

This automatically sets the order of future interviews. Once the interviews are over, you can change the "Last interview" date and the table will be updated after a new sorting.

LET'S MEET

The tool we are developing will be used on a daily basis to better anticipate upcoming interviews.

We can then integrate today's date to compare future interview dates with today.

To insert today's date in a cell, simply write "=TODAY()" and see what happens. When you open your file tomorrow, the cell will be on tomorrow's date.

For the purposes of this project, we'll insert the following values in cells G1 and H1:

We estimate that it's 11/02/2023, so a real application would require you to enter "=TODAY()" in H1.

LET'S MEET

The current date can be used to indicate the urgency of upcoming interviews.

Select column F, then click on "Conditional formatting - New rule" :

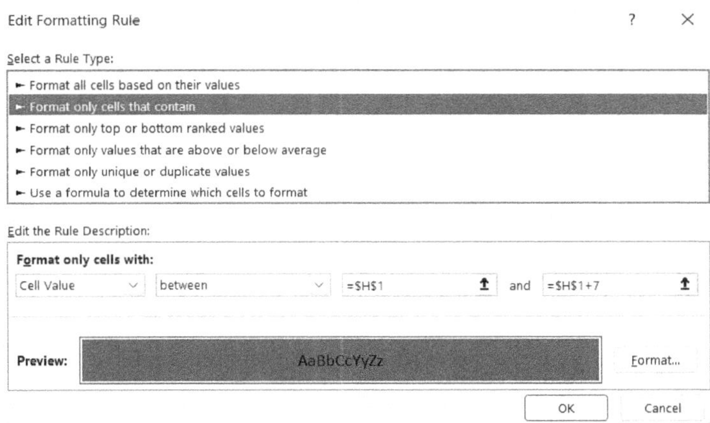

Dates between today's date (H1) and today's date + one week (H1 + 7) will appear in red.

Here, we'll make 3 rules:
- **Date within 7 days: red box**
- **Date in 7 to 15 days: orange box**
- **Date more than 15 days away: green box.**

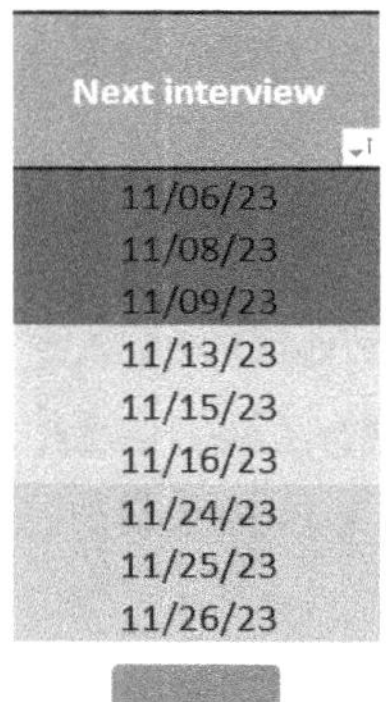

LET'S MEET

Now that our workbook is up and running, we can add some facilitating functions.

Management has asked us to change the interval between interviews for department heads: we therefore need to modify this in the "Interview information" sheet.

We're going to create a button to access the sheet quickly. Click on Insert - Shapes :

Right-click on the shape, then "Link": you can choose the document sheet to which you want to link the button:

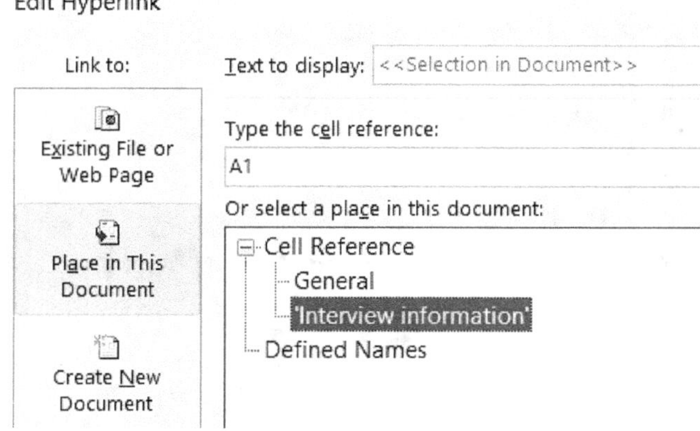

In the "Interview information" sheet, create a "Back to General" button using the same procedure.

LET'S MEET

You've just completed the workbook, but it will be stored on a shared folder.

As this information is sensitive, access must be password-protected.

Go to "File" then "Info" and "Encrypt with password" :

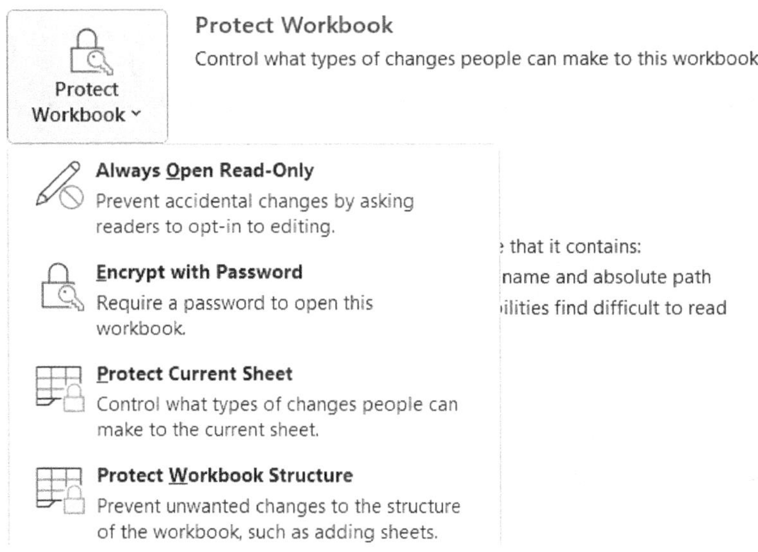

Choose a password, and that's it!

WHERE DOES THE MONEY GO?

This project will take you into the realm of concepts you've probably heard of: pivot tables. You'll start with a file containing expense reports collected from your employees; we're going to analyze where these expenses are spent.

The base file is "05 - Subject Expense reports.xlsx".

An example of a correction is the file :
"05 - Expense reports.xlsx"

PT = PivotTable
PC = PivotChart

Open the basic file, and you're ready to go!

	A	B	C	D	E
1	Name	Department	Nature	Date	Amount
2	Leonidas Malone	Maintenance	Fuel	02/26/23	29
3	Tobias Seton	Marketing	Toll	05/05/22	37
4	Greyson Mccarty	Maintenance	Fuel	04/05/22	74
5	Armando Stein	Marketing	Toll	10/22/22	22
6	Tobias Seton	Marketing	Restaurant	07/20/23	64
7	Luis Mullins	Production	Toll	11/10/24	61
8	Leonidas Malone	Maintenance	Toll	07/27/22	29
9	Gerardo Delgado	Marketing	Fuel	06/20/22	53
10	Camden Bishop	Marketing	Restaurant	04/09/24	39
11	Myles Brock	Marketing	Fuel	01/03/23	24
12	Luis Mullins	Production	Toll	03/21/22	40
13	Camden Bishop	Marketing	Hotel	02/05/24	80
14	Armando Stein	Marketing	Toll	01/25/22	35
15	Gerardo Delgado	Marketing	Hotel	02/21/23	29
16	Finley Noel	Production	Restaurant	08/31/24	45
17	Odin Hancock	Maintenance	Restaurant	12/14/24	60

Covered concepts :
Tables, pivot tables, slicers, pivot charts.

WHERE DOES THE MONEY GO?

To begin with, let's create a table via "Insert - Table", with the headers already filled in.

	A	B	C	D	E
1	**Name**	**Department**	**Nature**	**Date**	**Amount**
2	Leonidas Malone	Maintenance	Fuel	02/26/23	29
3	Tobias Seton	Marketing	Toll	05/05/22	37
4	Greyson Mccarty	Maintenance	Fuel	04/05/22	74
5	Armando Stein	Marketing	Toll	10/22/22	22
6	Tobias Seton	Marketing	Restaurant	07/20/23	64
7	Luis Mullins	Production	Toll	11/10/24	61
8	Leonidas Malone	Maintenance	Toll	07/27/22	29
9	Gerardo Delgado	Marketing	Fuel	06/20/22	53
10	Camden Bishop	Marketing	Restaurant	04/09/24	39
11	Myles Brock	Marketing	Fuel	01/03/23	24
12	Luis Mullins	Production	Toll	03/21/22	40
13	Camden Bishop	Marketing	Hotel	02/05/24	80
14	Armando Stein	Marketing	Toll	01/25/22	35
15	Gerardo Delgado	Marketing	Hotel	02/21/23	29
16	Finley Noel	Production	Restaurant	08/31/24	45
17	Odin Hancock	Maintenance	Restaurant	12/14/24	60

We're going to create several sheets later, so we'll rename this one "DB" for "Database". Each time we create a new table or chart, we'll return to this sheet.

DB

WHERE DOES THE MONEY GO?

Select cell A1, then go to "Insert - PivotTable". A window will ask if the source of the table is the one you've just created, and if you want to create it in a new sheet. Click on "Ok".

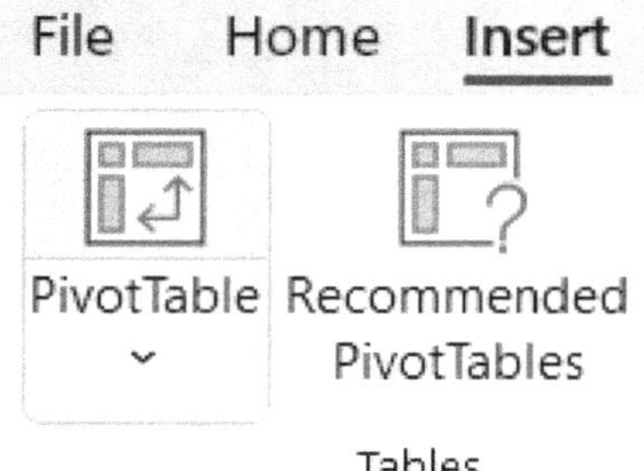

On the right-hand side of your screen, you can select the value fields to be displayed: choose " Department" " and " Amount before tax ". Your first PT is created.

Right-click on the amount values to transform them into $.

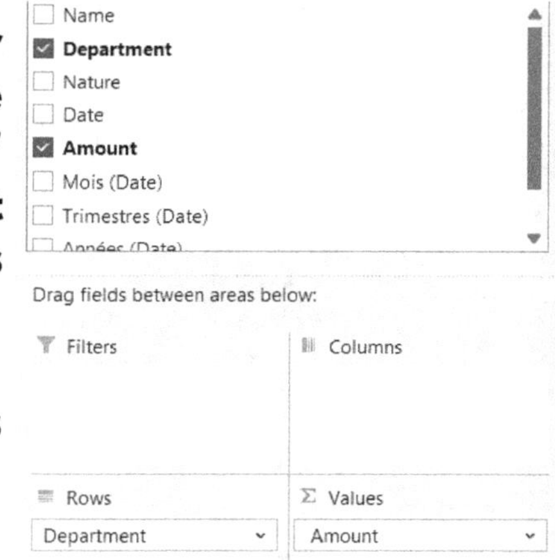

Row Labels	Amount
Maintenance	$ 32 294,00
Marketing	$ 50 703,00
Production	$ 21 195,00
Grand Total	**$ 104 192,00**

Rename the "PT by Department" sheet, rename the value field "Amount" and return to the "DB" sheet.

WHERE DOES THE MONEY GO?

As before, insert a new PT.

We're now going to display more value fields: Nature, Years and Amount. If the value fields don't fit in the right place, drag and drop them into the appropriate category.

Row Labels ▾	Amount
⊟ Fuel	**$24 999,00**
2022	$9 119,00
2023	$7 858,00
2024	$8 022,00
⊟ Toll	**$25 754,00**
2022	$8 193,00
2023	$8 508,00
2024	$9 053,00

Transform the values into $, rename the value field "Amount", rename the sheet "PT by nature and year" , and return to the " DB" sheet.

WHERE DOES THE MONEY GO?

As before, insert a new PT.

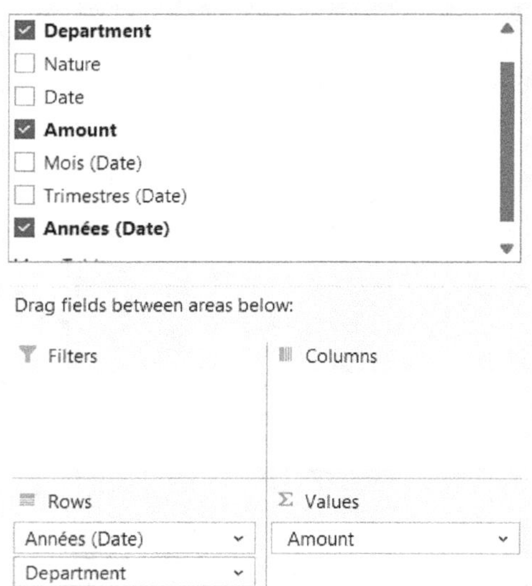

We're now going to display the year, department and amount value fields. Once the PT has been created, go to "Design" to change the style of your PT.

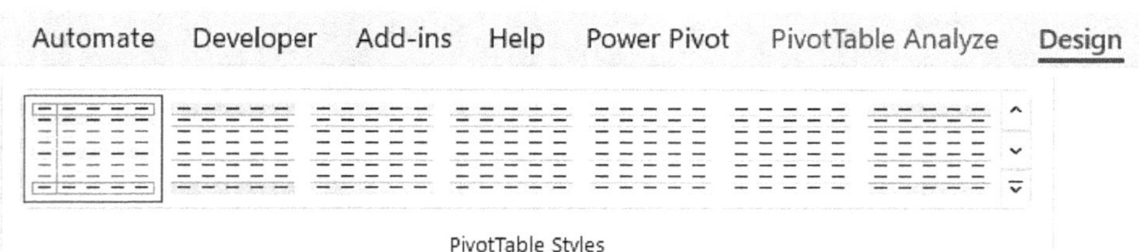

Transform the values into $, rename the value field "Amount", rename the sheet "PT by year and department", and stay in the sheet.

WHERE DOES THE MONEY GO?

It is possible to filter pivot tables using a tool called "Segments". Click on the PT, then "PivotTable Analyze", "Insert Slicer".

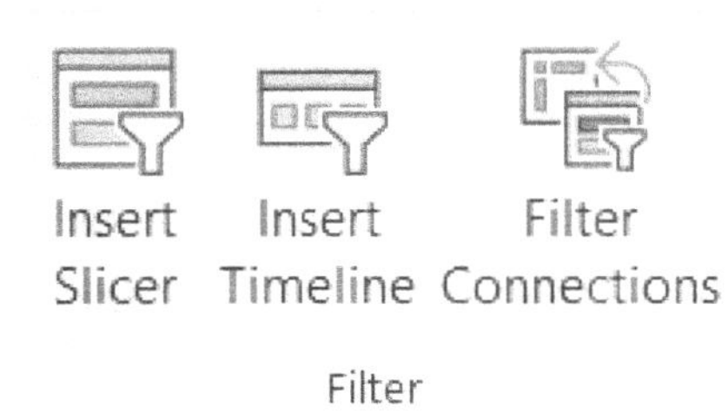

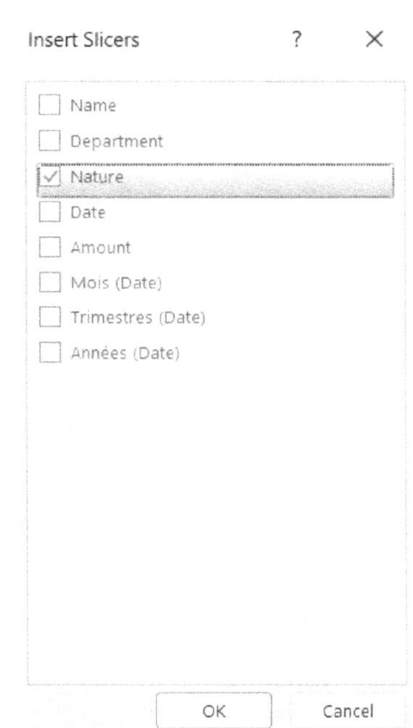

Select "Nature" in the window that appears.

Place the slicer next to the table, then click on the different categories to see your analysis evolve in real time.

Row Labels	Amount
2022	
Maintenance	$10 142,00
Marketing	$17 768,00
Production	$6 861,00
2023	
Maintenance	$11 474,00
Marketing	$16 271,00
Production	$6 913,00
2024	
Maintenance	$10 678,00
Marketing	$16 664,00
Production	$7 421,00
Grand Total	**$104 192,00**

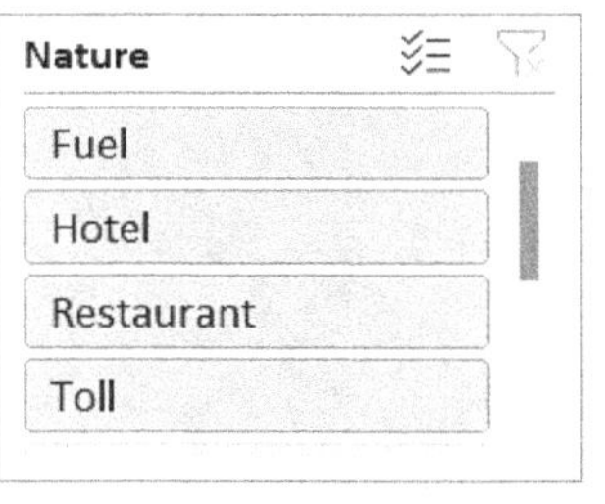

Now return to the "DB" sheet.

WHERE DOES THE MONEY GO?

Select cell A1, then go to "Insert - PivotChart". A window asks if the source of the table is the one you've just created, and if you want to create it in a new sheet.
Click on "Ok".

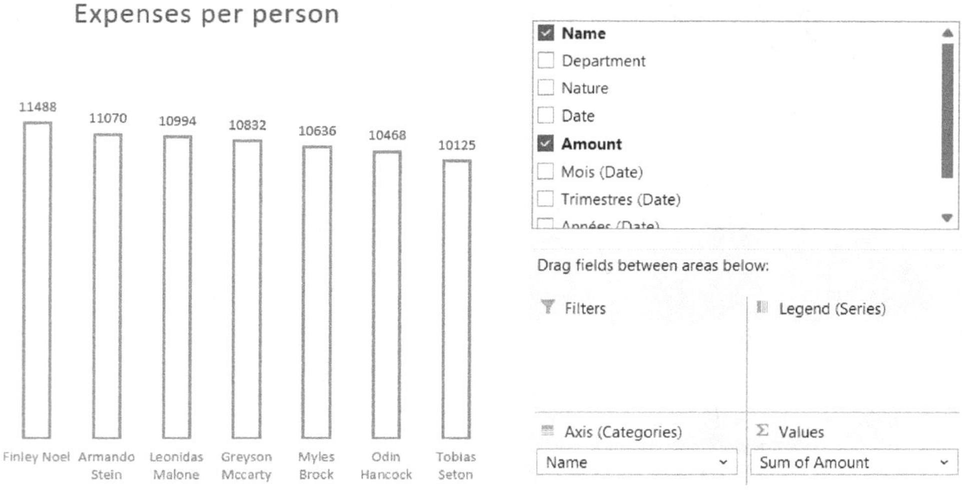

PivotChart

On the right-hand side of your screen, you can select the value fields to be displayed: choose "Name" and "Amount before tax". Your first PC is created.

On the PT created in parallel, right-click on the amounts and then "Sort": your chart will then show the order. You can also transform the values into $.

Rename the sheet "PC per person" , explore the graph layouts and return to the "DB" sheet.

WHERE DOES THE MONEY GO?

As before, insert a new PC.

Its purpose is to show the amount of expenses over the years: in this way, a line will be requested.

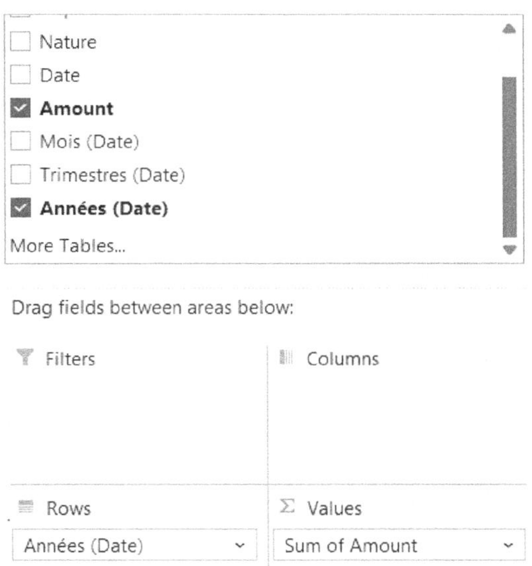

Amounts in $ should appear on this line.

Rename the sheet "PC by year" , explore the graph layouts and return to the "DB" sheet.

WHERE DOES THE MONEY GO?

As before, insert a new PC.

The purpose of this is to show the amount of expenses according to their nature: in this way, a Pie Chart will be requested.

The chart should show the percentages and the nature of the expense.

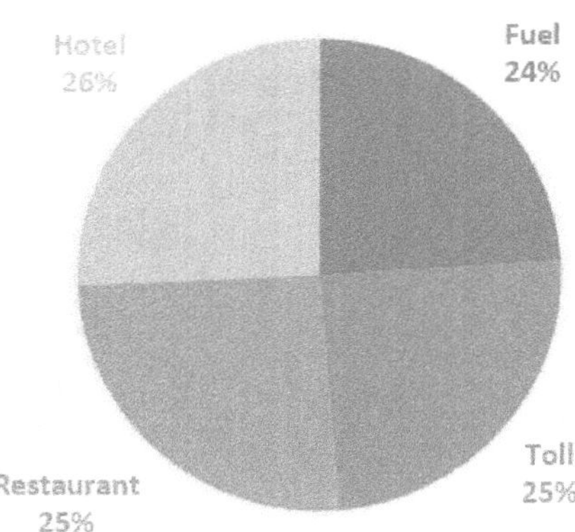

Rename the sheet "PC by nature" , explore the graph layouts and return to the "DB" sheet.

WHERE DOES THE MONEY GO?

As before, insert a new PC.

Its purpose is to show the amount of expenses by department: in this way, a column chart is requested.

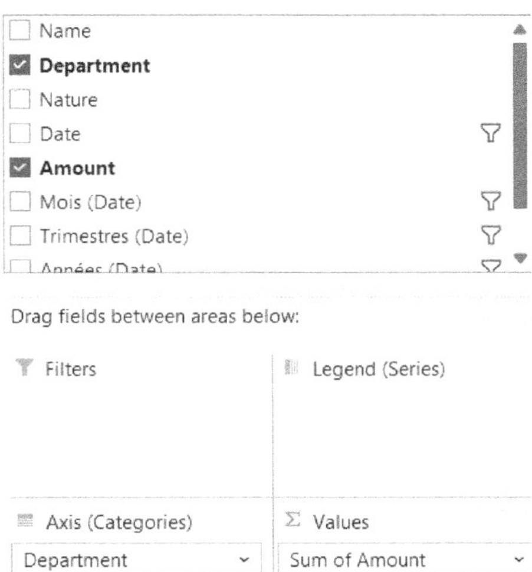

This chart should show services and amounts in $ sorted in descending order.

Rename the sheet "PC by department", explore the graph layouts and stay on this sheet.

WHERE DOES THE MONEY GO?

In the "Pivot chart analyze" section, which appears after clicking on the chart, we can insert not only a slicer, but also a timeline:

Place your timeline next to your graph, and change the dates; your graph automatically updates to include the requested period.

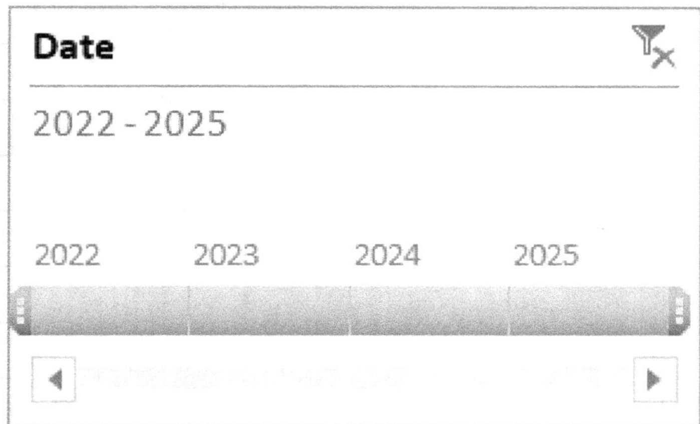

SPORT MARKET

Today's the big day: you've been hired as a data analyst for a sporting goods franchise. The objective will be to analyze sales across the globe.

The base file is "06 - Subject Sporting Goods Store.xlsx".

An example of a correction is the file :
"06 - Sporting goods store.xlsx"

Open the basic file, and you're off!

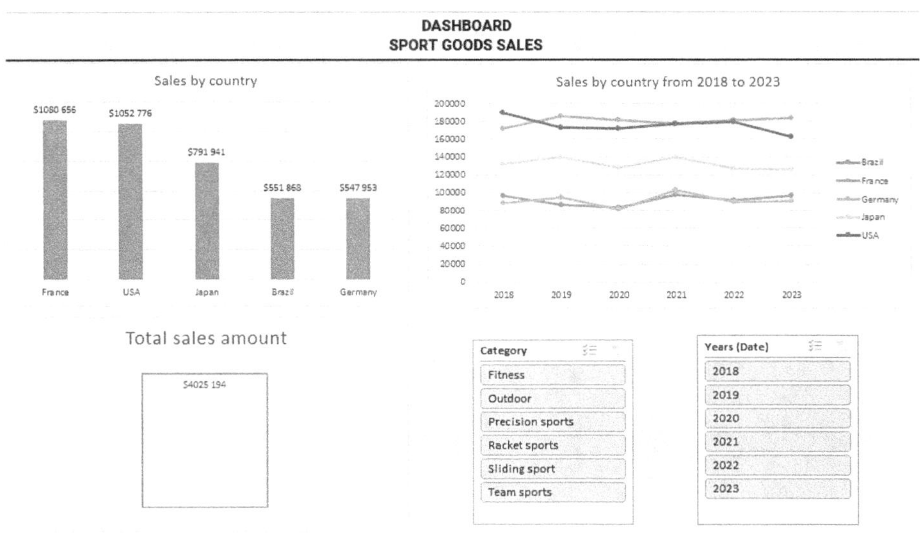

Concepts covered :
Tables, pivot tables, percentages, pivot charts, slicers.

SPORT MARKET

As usual, the first step is to transform the data into a table for ease of use.

Date	Purchase number	Category	Subcategory	Country	City	Amount
12/04/20	122263	Sliding sport	Roller skating	France	Marseille	69
11/16/20	79076	Fitness	Accessories	France	Marseille	6
05/08/19	143132	Team sports	Volleyball	France	Paris	61
10/03/23	24676	Team sports	Basketball	France	Paris	156
02/26/23	95606	Sliding sport	Snowboarding	Japan	Kyoto	282
01/08/22	144287	Fitness	Dumbbells	Brazil	Brasilia	31
09/17/23	60306	Sliding sport	Skiing	USA	New York	402
06/22/18	165332	Fitness	Accessories	Brazil	Rio de Janeiro	10
10/03/23	52224	Fitness	Accessories	Germany	Munich	3
08/26/23	116994	Sliding sport	Roller skating	Japan	Kyoto	56
12/24/23	195272	Sliding sport	Skateboarding	France	Lyon	24
03/17/22	101239	Racket sports	Badminton	Brazil	Rio de Janeiro	65
01/22/21	58874	Sliding sport	Snowboarding	USA	Miami	288
10/10/20	129579	Outdoor	Water sports	Germany	Berlin	110
12/25/20	164084	Team sports	Handball	USA	Chicago	125
10/10/18	125166	Sliding sport	Surfing	Germany	Berlin	342

The headers are already filled in, and work can be done on the data types, but this is not essential.

SPORT MARKET

Create an initial PT in a new sheet, containing the category, sub-category and amount.

Row Labels	Amount
⊟ **Sliding sport**	**$1 117 304**
Skiing	$378 770
Surfing	$359 431
Snowboarding	$273 351
Roller skating	$63 989
Skateboarding	$41 763
⊟ **Precision sports**	**$926 036**
Golf	$814 587
Archery	$111 449
⊟ **Outdoor**	**$757 910**
Camping	$563 361
Water sports	$173 389
Rock climbing	$21 160
⊟ **Team sports**	**$536 703**
Football	$175 061
Basketball	$147 645
Handball	$135 815
Volleyball	$78 182

The "Amount" field can be renamed, and the values converted to $. In addition, the table must be sorted in descending order (right-click on a category, then sort).

Rename the sheet "PT category":

PT category

SPORT MARKET

In the same table, let's drag and drop the "Amount" field back into the values:

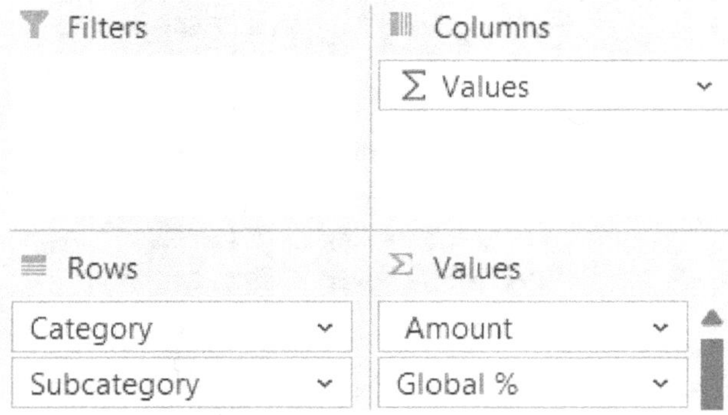

Access the Value Field settings, then rename the "global %" and choose "% of Grand total" from the "Show values as" drop-down list:

Row Labels	Amount	Global %
⊟ **Sliding sport**	**$1 117 304**	**27,76%**
Skiing	$378 770	9,41%
Surfing	$359 431	8,93%
Snowboarding	$273 351	6,79%
Roller skating	$63 989	1,59%
Skateboarding	$41 763	1,04%
⊟ **Precision sports**	**$926 036**	**23,01%**
Golf	$814 587	20,24%
Archery	$111 449	2,77%
⊟ **Outdoor**	**$757 910**	**18,83%**
Camping	$563 361	14,00%
Water sports	$173 389	4,31%
Rock climbing	$21 160	0,53%

Percentages are now created.

SPORT MARKET

In the same table, let's drag and drop the "Amount" field back into the values:

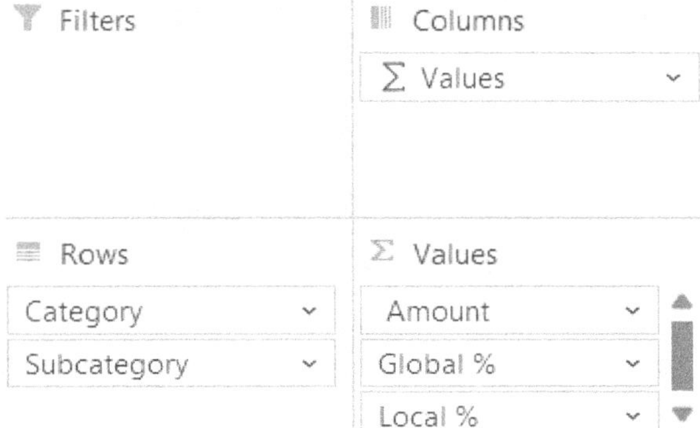

Access the value field parameters, then rename it "Local %" and choose "% of parent total" from the "Show values as" drop-down list:

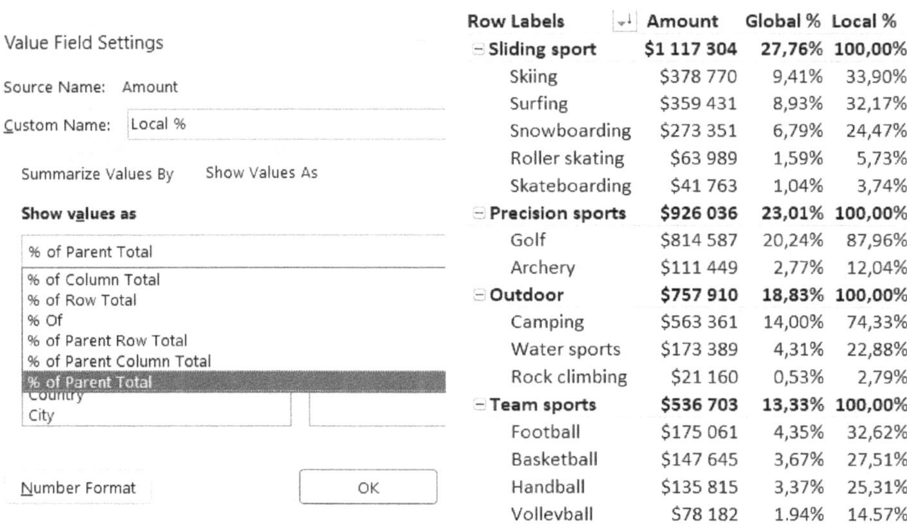

Local percentages are now created for each category: please note that if the parent is selected incorrectly, the percentages will not appear. Here, the parent is the category. Let's return to the initial sheet.

SPORT MARKET

Create another PT in a new sheet, containing the country, city and amount.

Row Labels	Amount
⊖ France	$1 080 656
Bordeaux	$271 189
Lyon	$254 586
Marseille	$271 331
Paris	$283 550
⊖ USA	$1 052 776
Chicago	$274 276
Los Angeles	$268 584
Miami	$220 443
New York	$289 473
⊖ Japan	$791 941
Kyoto	$262 509
Osana	$245 879
Tokyo	$283 553
⊖ Brazil	$551 868
Brasilia	$302 125
Rio de Janeiro	$249 743
⊖ Germany	$547 953
Berlin	$304 698
Munich	$243 255
Grand Total	$4 025 194

The "Amount" field can be renamed, and the values converted to $. In addition, the table must be sorted in descending order (right-click on a country, then sort).

Rename the sheet "PT by country":

PT by country

SPORT MARKET

In the same table, let's drag and drop the "Amount" field back into the values:

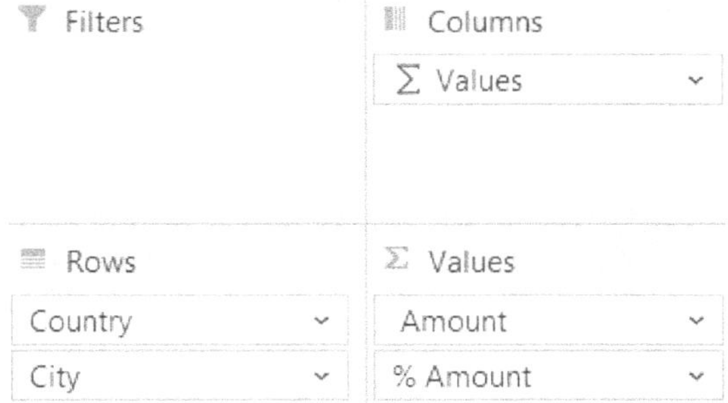

Access the value field parameters, then rename it "'% Amount" and choose "% of Parent Row Total" from the "'Show Values as" drop-down list:

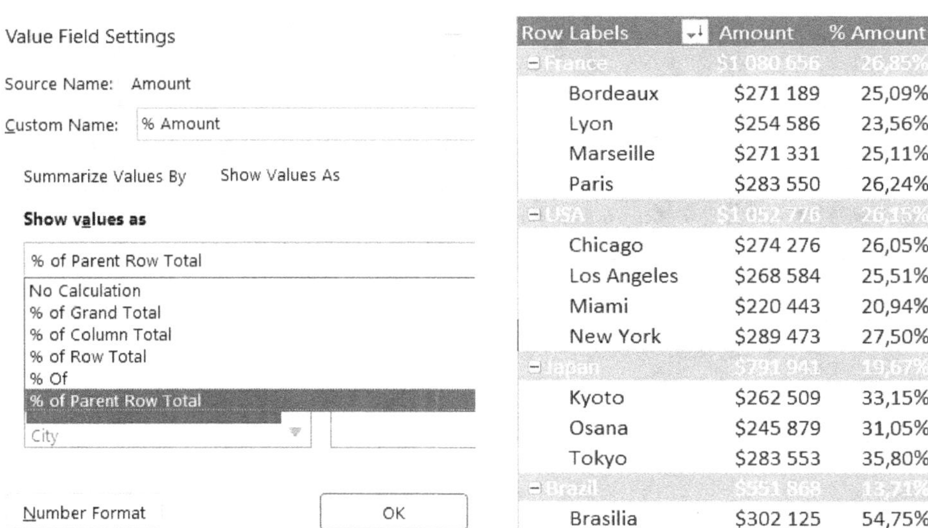

This percentage category is a combination of the previous two: the total percentage appears on the countries, and each has its own country-specific detail. Now return to the initial sheet.

SPORT MARKET

The aim here is to create a dashboard containing several dynamic pivot charts in a "Dashboard" sheet.

Create a PC in a new sheet, containing the country and the amount.

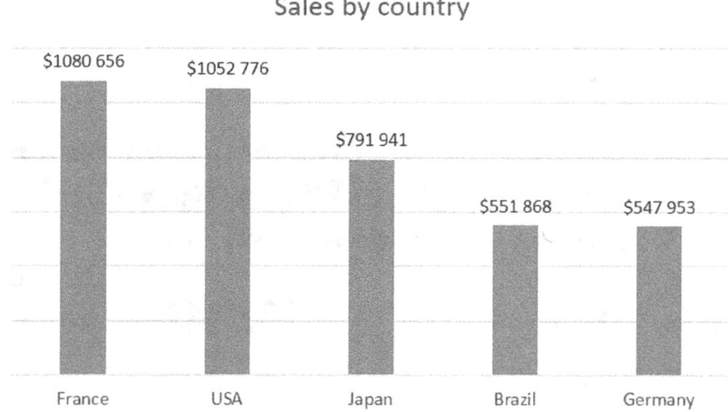

The "Amount" field can be converted to $. In addition, the chart must be sorted in descending order (right-click on a country in the table, then sort). Insert the title and labels for the amounts, and clear the chart.

Rename the sheet "Dashboard":

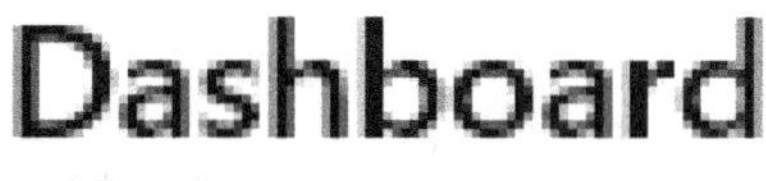

Now return to the initial sheet.

SPORT MARKET

Create a PC in the "Dashboard" sheet, containing the country, date and amount.

The exercise here is to work with the value fields so that the information appears in the same format as the one proposed.

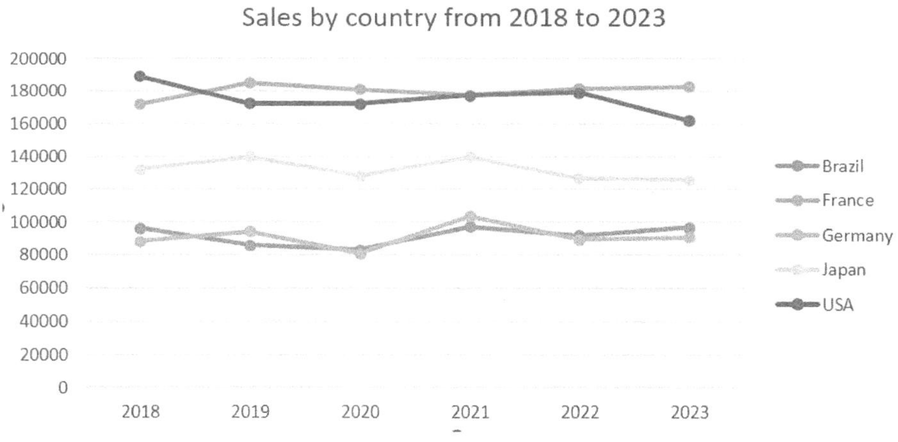

In the dashboard, position this chart so that it aligns with the previous one.

Note: the background of the dashboard can be a grey fill to make the charts stand out better.

Now return to the initial sheet.

SPORT MARKET

Create a PC in the "Dashboard" sheet, containing only the amount.

The exercise here is to find the best format for this indicator, which will be highlighted in the dashboard:

Total sales amount

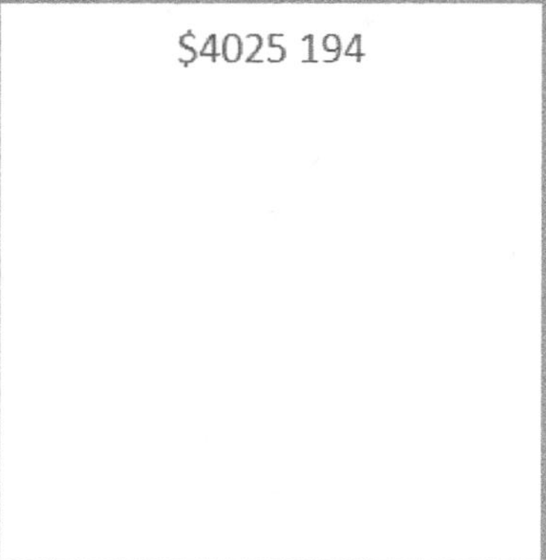

The chart should be purged (removing unnecessary elements), with the title and total amount highlighted.

In the dashboard, place this chart below the previous ones.

Stay on the "Dashboard" sheet for finishing touches.

SPORT MARKET

The aim here is to insert two slicers that can interact with all the graphs.

Click on a chart, then insert the "Category" and "Year" segments

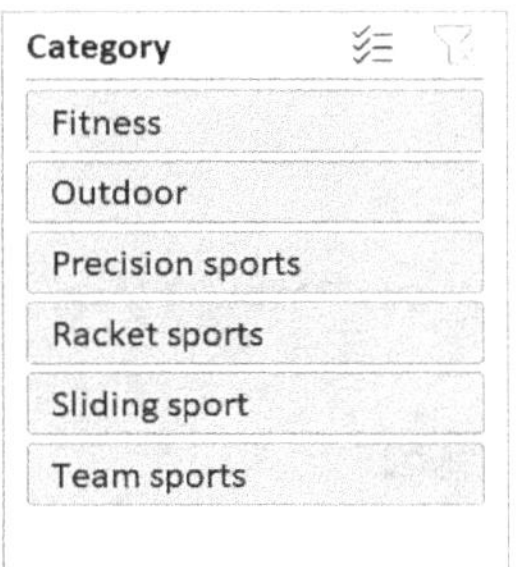

Click on the "Category" segment, then "Report connection" :

Report
Connections

Select the other charts on the page, click on "Ok" and test your slicer: it should update all the indicators on the page.

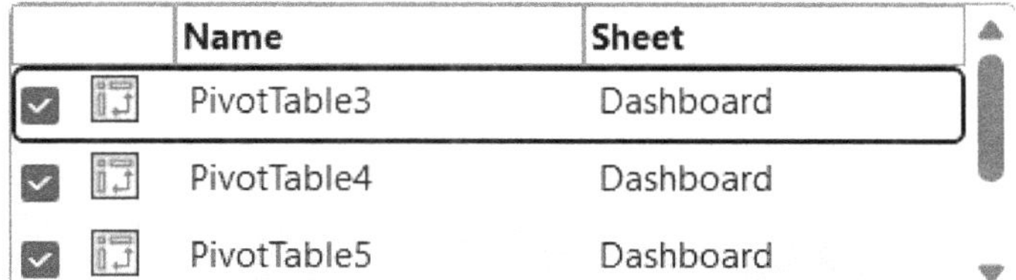

		Name	Sheet	
☑		PivotTable3	Dashboard	
☑		PivotTable4	Dashboard	
☑		PivotTable5	Dashboard	

Do the same for the years slicer.

To conclude this exercise, work on the formatting to make your dashboard as visual as possible.

REDUCE TYPING TIME

Starting with this project, we enter the world of VBA. You conduct studies to produce estimates, but it's time-consuming to copy/paste data from each sub-study to the final estimate. Let's automate it!

The basic file is "07 - Subject Study Summary.xlsx".

An example of a correction is the file:
"07 - Study summary.xlsm"

Don't hesitate to open the correction in parallel: future subjects are more complex than previous ones.

Open the basic file, and let's go!

STRUCTURABUILD

Study summary - Estimate	
Description	Price

Fill in prices

Delete prices

Covered concepts :
VBA code

REDUCE TYPING TIME

First of all, the "Developer" tab must be activated in Excel to access the VisualBasic section.

Click on File - Options - Customize Ribbon

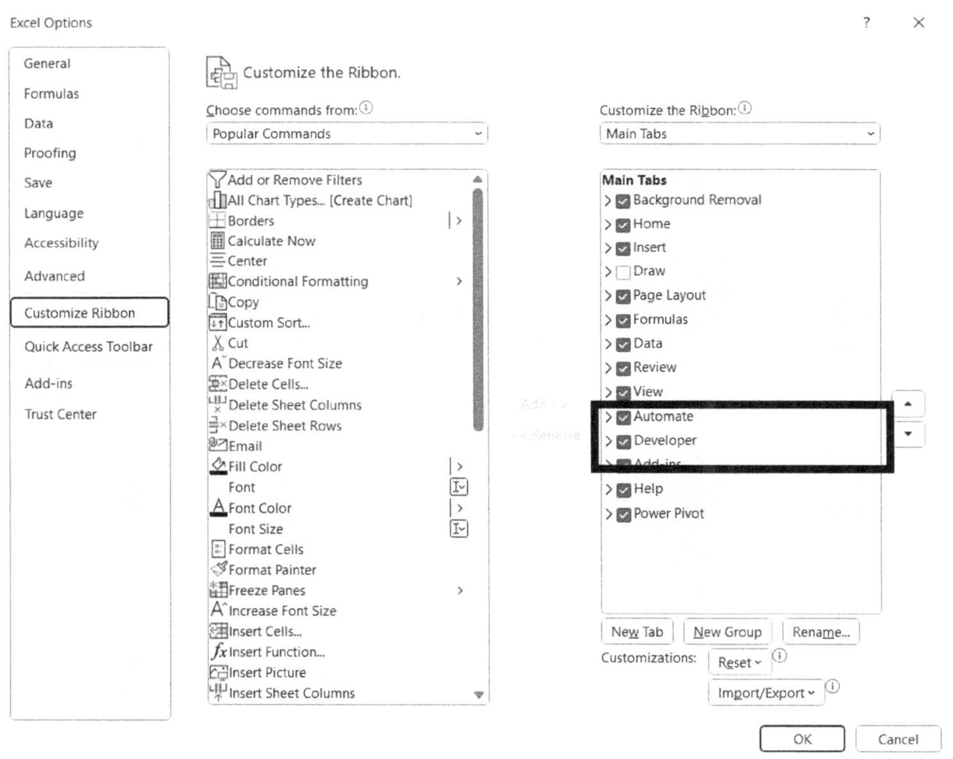

In the right-hand window, the "Developer" box must be ticked.

Exit the options and return to the initial sheet.

REDUCE TYPING TIME

Create forms called "Fill in prices" and "Delete prices" next to the final estimate:

These shapes will be used as buttons to trigger the Macros created afterwards: a Macro is a VBA program.

REDUCE TYPING TIME

We're now going to create our first VBA module.

Go to the "Developer" tab, then "Visual Basic" :

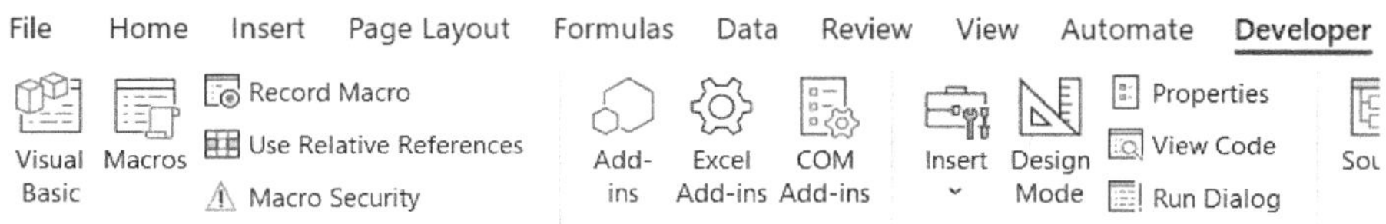

Once the Visual Basic window is open, click on Insert - Module to create the module containing the functions:

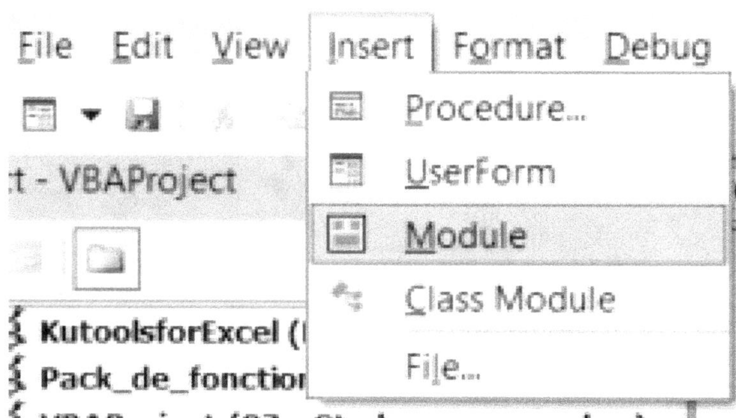

REDUCE TYPING TIME

Now we come to the most technical part of the book. Mastery of the elements seen above already takes you to a very interesting level, but this part represents an extra (big) step. I hope I haven't discouraged you!

If you're unfamiliar with the computer code, you can copy and paste it directly from the correction and understand the lines with the help of the explanations.

If errors appear, insert "MsgBox "Ok"" throughout your code to identify how far the execution has gone: the error given by Excel is not always the right one.

REDUCE TYPING TIME

First, we create the fillEstimate() function.

Here is the beginning of the code:

```
Sub fillEstimate()
    Application.ScreenUpdating = False
    Dim PageNum As Integer
    Dim Sheet As Worksheet
    Dim LastRow As Long
    Dim NextSheetExists As Boolean
```

These lines are used to declare the variables that will be used in the code:
- **PageNum will be the number of the page in which the data will be searched.**
- **Sheet will store the sub-study sheet.**
- **LastRow will be the last non-empty line, to identify the line on which we need to fill in the quote.**
- **NextSheetExists will be used to test the existence of the future sub-study, and stop the code if necessary.**

REDUCE TYPING TIME

A common practice in code is the use of loops.

In our case, we need to bring several prizes to the same place, so the same action will be performed several times in a row.

A loop is therefore suitable for repeating these actions (the pieces of code shown are not the final order, see page 77 for the complete code):

Start of loop :

```
Do While True
    NextSheetExists = SheetExists("Study" & PageNum)
```

End of loop :

```
        PageNum = PageNum + 1
    Loop
```

At the start of the loop, the function SheetExists is called. Here it is (it must be written outside the current function):

```
Function SheetExists(F As String) As Boolean
    On Error Resume Next
    SheetExists = Not Sheets(F) Is Nothing
End Function
```

REDUCE TYPING TIME

The test performed on the previous page provides a Boolean value: i.e. 0 or 1.

So, if the output value is 0, it means that the next page doesn't exist (example: test if page "Study7" exists when there are only 6 studies up to "Study6").

Here's the test:

```
If Not NextSheetExists Then
    Exit Do
End If
```

If the test is met, i.e. the sheet doesn't exist, then an exit from the loop and therefore the end of the code is executed (Exit Do).

REDUCE TYPING TIME

Here is the rest of the code, which will enable several elements detailed below:

```
Set Sheet = Sheets("Study" & PageNum)

RowNumberToFill = 8 + PageNum * 2

LastRow = Worksheets("Resume"). _
Cells(Rows.Count, "A").End(xlUp).Row

If RowNumberToFill > LastRow Then
    Worksheets("Resume"). _
    Rows(RowNumberToFill).Resize(2).Insert _
    Shift:=xlDown, CopyOrigin:=xlFormatFromLeftOrAbove
End If
```

- **Assignment of active sheet to variable Sheet**
- **Identification of line number to be filled**
- **Identification of last non-empty line**
- **Test: if line number to be filled is greater than last non-empty line, resize cells**

REDUCE TYPING TIME

The data to be transferred to the main quotation are the price and the description.

So, in the loop, we need to identify these values and "copy" them into the estimate:

```vba
' price insertion
 Worksheets("Resume").Cells(RowNumberToFill, "A").Value _
 = Worksheets("Study" & PageNum).Cells(1, 2).Value

 'Description insertion
 Worksheets("Resume").Cells(RowNumberToFill, "B").Value _
 = Worksheets("Study" & PageNum).Cells(15, 2).Value
```

For prices, the code designates the cell in the "Estimate" sheet to be filled in, then designates it as equal to the cell in the loop's current "Study" sheet.

The same process is used for the designation, only the cells designated are different.

REDUCE TYPING TIME

Here is the global code:

```vba
Sub fillEstimate()
    Application.ScreenUpdating = False
    Dim PageNum As Integer
    Dim Sheet As Worksheet
    Dim LastRow As Long
    Dim NextSheetExists As Boolean

    PageNum = 1

    Set Sheet = Nothing

    Do While True
        NextSheetExists = SheetExists("Study" & PageNum)

        If Not NextSheetExists Then
            Exit Do
        End If

        Set Sheet = Sheets("Study" & PageNum)

        RowNumberToFill = 8 + PageNum * 2

        LastRow = Worksheets("Resume"). _
        Cells(Rows.Count, "A").End(xlUp).Row

        If RowNumberToFill > LastRow Then
            Worksheets("Resume"). _
            Rows(RowNumberToFill).Resize(2).Insert _
            Shift:=xlDown, CopyOrigin:=xlFormatFromLeftOrAbove
        End If

        ' price insertion
        Worksheets("Resume").Cells(RowNumberToFill, "A").Value _
        = Worksheets("Study" & PageNum).Cells(1, 2).Value

        'Description insertion
        Worksheets("Resume").Cells(RowNumberToFill, "B").Value _
        = Worksheets("Study" & PageNum).Cells(15, 2).Value


        PageNum = PageNum + 1
    Loop

    Worksheets("Resume").Activate
End Sub
```

REDUCE TYPING TIME

Finally, you need to assign the Macro you've built to the button you created at the beginning. To do this, right-click on the button:

Select "Assign Macro..." then choose "fillEstimate" and click "Ok".

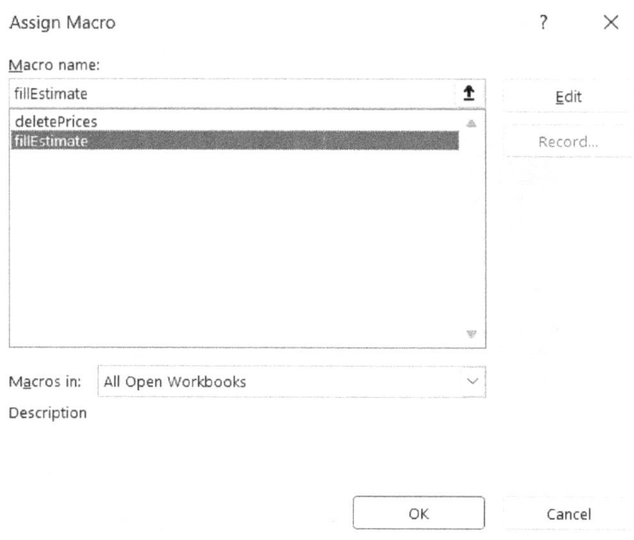

REDUCE TYPING TIME

A Macro must be created to delete the elements previously filled in.

Here is the code:

```
Sub deletePrices()

        Worksheets("Resume").Range("A9:B25").ClearContents

End Sub
```

This Macro selects the cells whose contents are to be deleted, and deletes them using "ClearContents".

As before, the Macro can be assigned to the "Delete prices" button.

In just two clicks, the estimate can be completed and purged!

REDUCE TYPING TIME

To conclude this project, it's important to save the file in the right format.

If the file is saved as .xlsx, then all the macros are deleted: you need to save it as .xlsm.

Go to File - Save as, then select .xlsm.

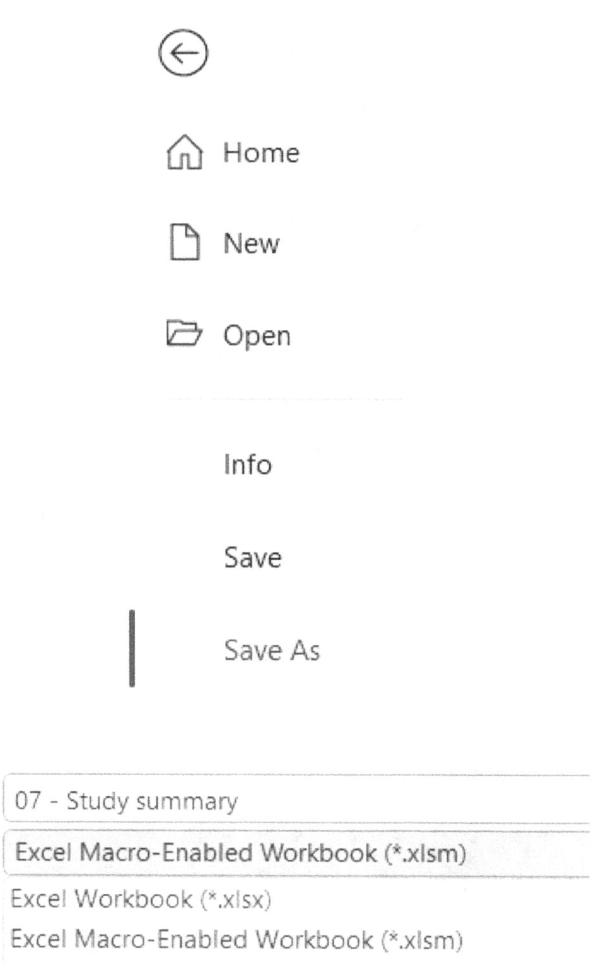

SIMPLY CLICK TO GENERATE A PDF

For this project, the base document is the previous file. Now that the document is complete, we'll automatically save it in PDF format.

The base file is "08 - Subject PDF.xlsm".

An example of a correction is the file :
"08 - PDF.xlsm"

Open the basic file, and you're good to go!

STRUCTURABUILD

Study summary - Estimate	
Description	Price

Fill in prices

Delete prices

Generate PDF

Covered concepts :
VBA code

SIMPLY CLICK TO GENERATE A PDF

The first step is to choose the folder that will receive your PDF file.

You can, for example, create a "Studies" folder on your desktop:

The path to this folder will be used later in the VBA code.

Be careful when manipulating VBA files with folders: many errors are caused by renamed folders, which cannot be found by the code...

SIMPLY CLICK TO GENERATE A PDF

The PDF you're about to generate will have a name, just like any other file.

However, we can't define a name that would be the same for each study; by default, the code would delete the old version of the PDF with the same name, and you'd only be able to keep the latest PDF.

So we're going to add two elements to our estimate on lines 33 and 34:

Customer	
Estimate number	2023-08-21

The customer's name must be filled in for each study to be included in the estimate name.

The quotation number is given by the =AUJOURDHUI() function, in YYYY-MM-DD format: in this way, PDFs are automatically sorted in chronological order.

SIMPLY CLICK TO GENERATE A PDF

Here is the complete code of the generatePDF() function:

```vba
Sub generatePDF()
Application.ScreenUpdating = False

PDF_NAME = ActiveSheet.Range("B34").Text & " " & _
ActiveSheet.Range("B33").Text

Range("A1:B39").Select
    Selection.ExportAsFixedFormat _
        Type:=xlTypePDF, _
        Filename:="C:\Users\nicoh\Desktop\Studies\" & _
        PDF_NAME, _
        Quality:=xlQualityStandard, _
        IncludeDocProperties:=True, _
        IgnorePrintAreas:=False, _
        OpenAfterPublish:=True

Worksheets("Resume").Range("B33").ClearContents


End Sub
```

The first line "Application.ScreenUpdating = False" indicates that when the function is executed, the screen does not update at each step: this gives a pleasant "software" effect at runtime.

```vba
Application.ScreenUpdating = False
```

SIMPLY CLICK TO GENERATE A PDF

As mentioned above, the name of the PDF will have to change with each edition.

So, to create it, we need to call on variables that will have different values each time the code is run.

```
PDF_NAME = ActiveSheet.Range("B34").Text & " " & _
ActiveSheet.Range("B33").Text
```

Here, the PDF name is composed of :
- Today's date inverted ...
- ... and the customer's name

The limit of this code arise if it's necessary to produce two estimates on the same day for the same customer: to counter this, you can add the time (=NOW)) to the PDF name, and duplication will then be impossible.

SIMPLY CLICK TO GENERATE A PDF

To generate a PDF, you need to tell the code which cell range will be converted.

This is the following line:

```
Range("A1:B39").Select
```

This is the cell range containing the estimate to be edited.

Next, indicate the type of format to which the PDF will be exported:

```
Type:=xlTypePDF, _
Filename:="C:\Users\nicoh\Desktop\Studies\"
```

This set of lines also contains the path to future file storage: this can be copied directly into the folder, then pasted into the code. Please note: a "\" must be added at the end for execution to work.

SIMPLY CLICK TO GENERATE A PDF

Other properties about the PDF can be specified: most are optional:

```
Quality:=xlQualityStandard, _
IncludeDocProperties:=True, _
IgnorePrintAreas:=False, _
OpenAfterPublish:=True
```

Here, for example, the quality of the future PDF will be standard, and the PDF will be asked to open after saving.

SIMPLY CLICK TO GENERATE A PDF

To conclude the code, deleting the customer's name can also be automated. Here's the line:

```
Worksheets("Resume").Range("B33").ClearContents
```

All that remains is to connect the Macro to a "Generate PDF" button created after the others.

With a simple click, you can save your documents directly in the folder you want!

SEND AN E-MAIL INSTANTLY

For this last project, the basic document is again the previous one; the aim is to generate an e-mail automatically with the PDF attached. Outlook must be installed and running on your computer for this code to run.

The basic file is "09 - Subject mails.xlsm".

An example of a correction is the file :
"09 - Mail.xlsm"

Open the basic file, and let's go!

Subject   Estimate No 2023-08-21

2023-08-21 Productivityguy.pdf
100 KB

Hello,

Please find attached our quote.

Thank you

Regards

Covered concepts :
VBA code

SEND AN E-MAIL INSTANTLY

To begin with, you need to authorize the connection with the Outlook application.
To do this, open the Visual Basic window, then Tools - References ...

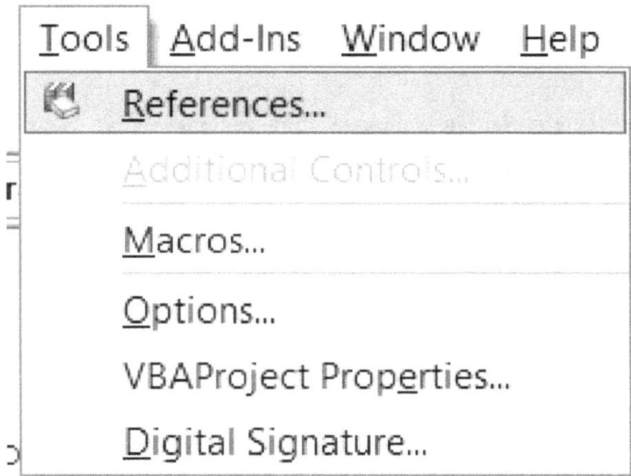

All applications related to Microsoft Outlook must be checked :

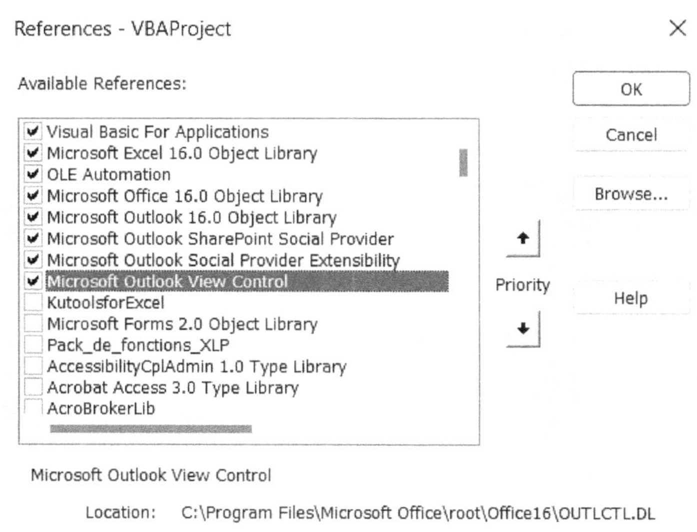

SEND AN E-MAIL INSTANTLY

The e-mail generation code will be directly integrated into the generatePDF() macro, so a single run will save the PDF and generate the e-mail.

The overall code is given on page 95; here's a detailed description of each part:

```
Dim appOutlook As Outlook.Application
    Set appOutlook = Outlook.Application
    Dim MESSAGE As Outlook.MailItem
    Dim objRecipient As Outlook.Recipient

    Set MESSAGE = appOutlook.CreateItem(olMailItem)
    With MESSAGE
```

The first part explains how to use the Outlook application, and how to create a message.

SEND AN E-MAIL INSTANTLY

The message can be customized using VBA: this saves a great deal of time when writing e-mails.

First of all, here's the line for inserting a subject to the e-mail you've created:

```
.Subject = "Estimate No " & ActiveSheet.Range("B34").Text
```

The subject name will be "Estimate No." followed by the current date cell inverted YYYY-MM-DD: in this way, the subject is specific to the estimate.

Here's the body of the e-mail:

```
.BodyFormat = olFormatPlain
.Body = "Hello," & vbCr & vbCr & _
"Please find attached our quote." & vbCr & vbCr & _
"Thank you" & vbCr & vbCr & _
"Regards"
```

The .Body allows you to write the e-mail directly beforehand. The "vbCr" formula lets you make line breaks in the body of the final e-mail.

SEND AN E-MAIL INSTANTLY

The e-mail created must contain the PDF attachment created earlier. The action of adding an attachment manually will then be eliminated.

Here's the code that makes this possible:

```
Dim MaPJ
MaPJ = "C:\Users\nicoh\Desktop\Studies\" & PDF_NAME & ".pdf"
```

The attachment is stored in a variable. We notice that the **PDF_NAME** used previously is used again, to get the freshly created PDF.

After checking that the attachment exists, it is added to the e-mail:

```
If Dir(MaPJ) <> "" Then
    .Attachments.Add MaPJ
End If
```

SEND AN E-MAIL INSTANTLY

To conclude this code, a read receipt is added, and the code is asked to display the e-mail:

```
.ReadReceiptRequested = True


.Display
```

Here is the complete code:

```
Dim appOutlook As Outlook.Application
    Set appOutlook = Outlook.Application
    Dim MESSAGE As Outlook.MailItem
    Dim objRecipient As Outlook.Recipient

    Set MESSAGE = appOutlook.CreateItem(olMailItem)
    With MESSAGE


    .Subject = "Estimate No " & ActiveSheet.Range("B34").Text


    .BodyFormat = olFormatPlain
    .Body = "Hello," & vbCr & vbCr & _
    "Please find attached our quote." & vbCr & vbCr & _
    "Thank you" & vbCr & vbCr & _
    "Regards"



    Dim MaPJ
    MaPJ = "C:\Users\nicoh\Desktop\Studies\" & PDF_NAME & ".pdf"



    If Dir(MaPJ) <> "" Then
        .Attachments.Add MaPJ
    End If


    .ReadReceiptRequested = True


    .Display

    End With
```

SUMMARY OF CONCEPTS COVERED

Basic formulas

Calculating an average	**=AVERAGE(tested_range))**
Calculating a maximum	**=MAX(tested_range)**
Calculating a minimum	**=MIN(tested_range)**
Count a number of non-empty cells	**=COUNTA(tested_range)**
Showing values by testing cells	**=IF(Test ; Value if true ; Value if false)**
Point to a cell in a table	**=INDEX(array; Row n° ; Column n°)**
Designate the position of a value in a range	**=MATCH(lookup value ; lookup array; type)**

SUMMARY OF CONCEPTS COVERED

Basic formulas

Search for a value and return a value on the same line	=VLOOKUP(lookup value ; Table array ; column n° ; type)
Find a value and return an array on the same line	=XLOOKUP(lookup value ; lookup array ; return array)
Count the number of cells according to a criterion	=COUNTIF(range; criteria)
Sum cells according to criterion	=SUMIF(range; criteria; sumrange)
Insert multiple criteria	IFS : example =SUMIFS(...)
Invert table rows and columns	=TRANSPOSE(table)

SUMMARY OF CONCEPTS COVERED

Practical tools

Types of conditional formatting	Color scales, icons, everything is customizable.
Conditional formatting applications	Based on text, gaps between numbers, intervals, etc.
Tables	Insert - Table This feature makes it easy to use data, set up formulas and sort data.
Hyperlinks	To access a sheet of the document or another document, they can be assigned to a text, a shape ...

SUMMARY OF CONCEPTS COVERED

Tableaux croisés dynamiques

Value fields	Row, column, filter or value. Each characteristic of the table can be placed in one of these categories: make sure you choose the right one to obtain efficient tables!
Percentages	Percentages can be total on the column, or local on a category, or both. Applying parents opens up new reading possibilities.
Slicers	These are easy-to-use filters: placed next to a pivot table, they instantly filter the data; multiple elements can be selected within a segment (to study several years, for example).
Pivot Charts	Creating a graph necessarily generates a table in parallel: you need to choose visual displays that are relevant to the type of data being displayed.

SUMMARY OF CONCEPTS COVERED

Visual Basic code

Access the code	To create code, activate the "Developer" option and save your file as .xlsm.
Working in "project mode"	Code is an infinite subject with infinite possibilities. To progress, choose projects to work on and build your tools step by step.

Before you go...

Congratulations on your investment in this course! Mastering Excel is a highly prized asset in the professional world, whatever your sector.

To continue to progress, build on the files you're already using to integrate additional functions: it's in this logic of continuous improvement that you'll achieve remarkable performance.

Download link:
"https://www.wioptim.com/downloadexcel"